BEE-Friendly

A Comprehensive Guide to Home Beekeeping

Kiet Huynh

Table of Contents

Introduction

1. Welcome to Beekeeping

Beekeeping, or apiculture, is a fascinating and rewarding practice that has been part of human civilization for thousands of years. By deciding to become a beekeeper, you are joining a long tradition of individuals who have cared for bees and reaped the numerous benefits they offer. Whether you are interested in harvesting honey, beeswax, or simply contributing to the health of local ecosystems, beekeeping is an engaging and worthwhile endeavor.

In this chapter, we will introduce you to the world of beekeeping, covering the basics you need to know to get started. From understanding the crucial role bees play in our environment to the practical benefits of keeping bees at home, this section will set the foundation for your journey into apiculture.

1.1 The Importance of Bees

Bees are vital to the health of our planet and play a critical role in maintaining biodiversity and food production. Their importance cannot be overstated, and understanding their role in the ecosystem is the first step in appreciating the value of beekeeping.

Pollination and Food Production

One of the most significant contributions of bees is their role in pollination. Pollination is the process by which pollen is transferred from the male parts of a flower (anthers) to the female parts (stigma), resulting in fertilization and the production of seeds and fruits. While wind and other animals can assist in pollination, bees are among the most effective pollinators due to their behavior and physiology.

Approximately one-third of the food we consume depends on pollination by bees and other pollinators. This includes many fruits, vegetables, nuts, and seeds. Crops like apples, almonds, blueberries, cherries, avocados, cucumbers, and pumpkins rely heavily on bee pollination. Without bees, the yields of these crops would be significantly reduced, leading to decreased availability and higher prices of many foods we enjoy.

Moreover, bees contribute to the production of forages, such as clover and alfalfa, which are used to feed livestock. This indirectly supports the meat and dairy industries. In essence, bees are essential for the sustainability of our food systems.

Biodiversity and Ecosystem Health

Bees are not only crucial for agriculture but also for maintaining the health of wild ecosystems. Many wild plants depend on bees for pollination. These plants provide food and habitat for a variety of other wildlife, including birds, mammals, and insects. By supporting plant reproduction, bees help sustain the diversity of plant and animal life in their ecosystems.

The loss of bee populations can lead to a decline in plant species that depend on bee pollination, which in turn affects the animals that rely on those plants. This can create a cascading effect, disrupting entire ecosystems. Therefore, protecting and supporting bee populations is critical for the health and resilience of natural environments.

Economic Value

The economic value of bees extends beyond the direct products they provide, such as honey and beeswax. Pollination services by bees contribute billions of dollars to the global economy each year. In the United States alone, the economic value of bee pollination is estimated to be over $15 billion annually.

Farmers rely on healthy bee populations to ensure the productivity of their crops. Some even rent honeybee colonies during the blooming season to enhance pollination. This practice, known as migratory beekeeping, highlights the significant demand for pollination services and the economic importance of bees.

Environmental Indicators

Bees are also important environmental indicators, meaning their health reflects the state of the environment. Because bees are sensitive to changes in their surroundings, declines in bee populations can signal broader environmental issues, such as pesticide use, habitat loss, and climate change.

Monitoring bee health can provide valuable insights into the health of ecosystems and the impact of human activities on the environment. By paying attention to bees, we can better understand and address environmental challenges, ultimately leading to more sustainable practices and policies.

The Honey Bee Colony Structure

Understanding the structure of a honey bee colony provides insight into the complex and efficient nature of these insects. A typical colony consists of three types of bees: the queen, worker bees, and drones.

- *The Queen Bee:* The queen is the only fertile female in the colony and is responsible for laying all the eggs. She can lay up to 2,000 eggs per day during peak season. The queen also produces pheromones that help regulate the colony's activities and maintain social order.

- *Worker Bees:* Worker bees are infertile females and make up the majority of the colony. They perform various tasks throughout their lives, including foraging for nectar and pollen, feeding the queen and larvae, cleaning and protecting the hive, and producing honey and beeswax. Their roles change as they age, demonstrating a highly organized division of labor.

- Drones: Drones are male bees whose primary function is to mate with a virgin queen. They do not have stingers and do not participate in foraging or hive maintenance. After mating, drones die, and those that do not mate are often expelled from the hive before winter.

The Lifecycle of a Honey Bee

The lifecycle of a honey bee consists of four stages: egg, larva, pupa, and adult. This process is known as complete metamorphosis and takes about 21 days for worker bees, 24 days for drones, and 16 days for queens.

1. Egg: The queen lays eggs in individual cells within the hive. Each egg is about the size of a pinhead and is attached to the cell's bottom.

2. Larva: After three days, the egg hatches into a larva. Worker bees feed the larvae a diet of royal jelly initially, then transition to a mixture of pollen and honey known as "bee bread." Larvae grow rapidly and molt several times during this stage.

3. Pupa: Once the larva reaches a certain size, the cell is capped with beeswax, and the larva spins a cocoon around itself. It then enters the pupal stage, during which it undergoes significant transformation, developing wings, legs, and other adult structures.

4. Adult: After about 12 days in the pupal stage, the adult bee emerges from the cell. It starts its life as a young worker, performing tasks within the hive before eventually becoming a forager.

Threats to Bee Populations

Despite their importance, bee populations worldwide face numerous threats. Understanding these threats is essential for developing strategies to protect and support bees.

- *Pesticides:* Exposure to pesticides, particularly neonicotinoids, can be lethal to bees or impair their ability to forage, navigate, and reproduce. Pesticide contamination in pollen and nectar can also affect the health of the entire colony.

- *Habitat Loss:* Urbanization, agriculture, and other land uses can lead to the destruction of natural habitats that bees rely on for forage and nesting. Loss of floral diversity and continuous monoculture crops can limit the food sources available to bees.

- *Climate Change:* Changes in climate patterns can affect the availability of floral resources and the timing of bloom periods. Extreme weather events, such as droughts and floods, can also impact bee populations and their habitats.

- *Diseases and Parasites:* Bees are susceptible to various diseases and parasites, including the Varroa destructor mite, Nosema fungus, and American foulbrood bacteria. These pathogens and pests can weaken or decimate colonies if not properly managed.

- *Colony Collapse Disorder (CCD):* CCD is a phenomenon where the majority of worker bees in a colony disappear, leaving behind the queen, brood, and a few nurse bees. The exact cause of CCD is not fully understood, but it is believed to result from a combination of factors, including pesticide exposure, disease, and environmental stressors.

Conservation and Beekeeping Practices

Supporting bee populations involves both conservation efforts and sustainable beekeeping practices. Here are some key approaches to help bees thrive:

- *Habitat Restoration:* Planting a diversity of flowering plants, including native species, can provide bees with the forage they need. Creating green spaces, pollinator gardens, and wildflower meadows can help restore habitats for bees in urban and rural areas.

- *Pesticide Reduction:* Minimizing the use of pesticides, especially those harmful to bees, is crucial. Integrated pest management (IPM) practices that prioritize non-chemical control methods can reduce the impact on bee populations.

- *Sustainable Beekeeping:* Beekeepers can adopt practices that support bee health, such as providing adequate nutrition, monitoring for diseases and pests, and avoiding the overuse of chemical treatments. Maintaining genetic diversity in bee populations through breeding programs can also enhance resilience.

- *Education and Advocacy:* Raising awareness about the importance of bees and the threats they face is essential for garnering public support and driving policy changes. Beekeepers, educators, and conservationists can work together to promote bee-friendly practices and advocate for protective measures.

The Joy of Beekeeping

While the importance of bees and the challenges they face are critical to understand, beekeeping also offers numerous personal rewards. Many beekeepers find great joy and satisfaction in working with bees. The process of managing a hive, observing bee behavior, and harvesting honey can be incredibly fulfilling.

Beekeeping provides an opportunity to connect with nature and contribute to environmental conservation. It also fosters a sense of community, as beekeepers often share their experiences, knowledge, and products with others. Whether you are motivated by a love of nature, a desire for self-sufficiency, or a curiosity about these remarkable insects, beekeeping offers a unique and enriching experience.

Conclusion

The importance of bees extends far beyond their role in producing honey. They are essential for pollination, ecosystem health, and the economy. Understanding these roles helps us appreciate the value of bees and the significance of beekeeping. As you embark on your beekeeping journey, remember that you are not only gaining a rewarding hobby but also contributing to the preservation of these vital pollinators.

In the next sections of this book, we will delve deeper into the practical aspects of beekeeping, from setting up your apiary to managing your hive and harvesting honey. By learning and applying the principles of bee-friendly beekeeping, you can help ensure the health and sustainability of bee populations while enjoying the many benefits that come with being a beekeeper.

1.2 Benefits of Home Beekeeping

Home beekeeping offers numerous benefits that extend beyond simply producing honey. As you embark on this journey, you'll discover how beekeeping can positively impact your life, your garden, and the broader environment. This section delves into the multifaceted advantages of keeping bees at home.

Personal Satisfaction and Enjoyment

One of the most immediate benefits of home beekeeping is the personal satisfaction and enjoyment it brings. Beekeeping is a hobby that combines the beauty of nature with the satisfaction of caring for a living creature. Watching your bees thrive, observing their complex behaviors, and understanding the intricacies of their world can be incredibly rewarding.

For many, beekeeping becomes a meditative practice, a chance to disconnect from the fast-paced digital world and reconnect with nature. The rhythmic hum of a healthy hive and the simple, repetitive tasks associated with beekeeping can be soothing, reducing stress and promoting a sense of well-being.

Educational Opportunities

Beekeeping is a gateway to continuous learning. It offers a unique opportunity to delve into the fascinating world of entomology, biology, and ecology. Through beekeeping, you'll gain a deeper understanding of bee anatomy, behavior, and the crucial role bees play in ecosystems.

For families, beekeeping can be an educational tool for children, teaching them about responsibility, the environment, and the importance of biodiversity. Schools and community groups often use beekeeping projects to engage students in science, encouraging them to explore careers in environmental science, agriculture, and conservation.

Environmental Impact

One of the most significant benefits of home beekeeping is its positive impact on the environment. Bees are essential pollinators, responsible for the reproduction of many flowering plants and crops. By keeping bees, you contribute to local biodiversity and the health of ecosystems.

Pollination by bees enhances the productivity of gardens, orchards, and farms. This not only supports the growth of fruits, vegetables, and flowers but also helps maintain the genetic diversity of plants. In urban settings, where natural pollinators may be scarce, home beekeeping can significantly improve green spaces, parks, and gardens.

Additionally, beekeepers often become advocates for environmental stewardship. Through your work with bees, you'll likely develop a greater appreciation for the natural world and may take actions to protect habitats, reduce pesticide use, and promote sustainable practices in your community.

Health Benefits

The products of beekeeping offer numerous health benefits. Honey, a primary product, is not only a natural sweetener but also has medicinal properties. It contains antioxidants, vitamins, and minerals that can boost your immune system. Raw honey, in particular, is known for its antibacterial and anti-inflammatory properties, making it useful in treating wounds, soothing sore throats, and alleviating allergies.

Other bee products, such as propolis, royal jelly, and beeswax, also have health benefits. Propolis, a resin-like substance, has antimicrobial properties and is used in natural remedies and skincare products. Royal jelly, a nutrient-rich secretion, is believed to have anti-aging effects and can boost overall vitality. Beeswax is widely used in natural cosmetics and ointments, providing benefits for skin health.

Economic Benefits

Beekeeping can be economically rewarding. Besides producing honey for personal consumption, many beekeepers sell surplus honey and other bee products at local markets or online. High-quality, locally-produced honey often commands a premium price due to its unique flavors and health benefits.

Beekeepers can also sell beeswax, propolis, and royal jelly, diversifying their income streams. Additionally, offering pollination services to farmers and gardeners can be a lucrative business. As the demand for natural and locally-sourced products continues to rise, beekeeping presents numerous opportunities for entrepreneurial ventures.

Community and Social Benefits

Beekeeping fosters a sense of community. Many beekeepers join local beekeeping associations or clubs, where they can share experiences, gain knowledge, and receive support. These groups often organize workshops, field days, and social events, creating a network of like-minded individuals.

Community beekeeping projects can also bring people together, promoting cooperation and collective action. Urban beekeeping initiatives, for example, often involve community gardens, schools, and local organizations working together to create green spaces and support biodiversity.

Contribution to Scientific Research

Home beekeepers can contribute to scientific research and conservation efforts. Citizen science projects often rely on data collected by amateur beekeepers to monitor bee health, track environmental changes, and study the effects of pesticides and diseases on bee populations.

By participating in these projects, you can help scientists gather valuable information that can inform policies and practices aimed at protecting pollinators. Your observations and records of hive activity, bee behavior, and environmental conditions can provide insights that might otherwise be unavailable.

Enhancing Garden Productivity

Bees are exceptional pollinators, and their presence in your garden can significantly enhance the productivity of your plants. Fruits, vegetables, and flowers that depend on pollination will produce more abundant and higher-quality yields when bees are around.

For gardeners, this means a more bountiful harvest and a more vibrant, diverse garden. Plants that attract bees, such as flowering herbs, fruits, and ornamental flowers, will thrive, creating a beautiful and productive garden space.

Sustainable Living

Home beekeeping aligns with principles of sustainable living. By producing your own honey and bee products, you reduce your reliance on commercially produced goods, often reducing your carbon footprint. Beekeeping encourages you to adopt organic gardening practices, avoid pesticides, and create a more sustainable, eco-friendly lifestyle.

Furthermore, by supporting local ecosystems and promoting biodiversity, you contribute to the health and resilience of your local environment. Beekeeping can be a stepping stone to other sustainable practices, inspiring you to grow more of your own food, compost, and conserve resources.

Preserving Bee Populations

Beekeeping plays a crucial role in preserving bee populations, which are currently under threat from various factors, including habitat loss, pesticides, and disease. By maintaining healthy hives, you contribute to the survival of honey bees and other pollinators.

Your efforts in beekeeping help create a safer, more supportive environment for bees. This not only benefits your local area but also contributes to broader conservation efforts aimed at protecting these vital insects.

Mental and Physical Health Benefits

Beekeeping involves physical activity, from lifting hive boxes to managing frames, which can be beneficial for your physical health. The moderate exercise involved in beekeeping helps improve cardiovascular health, strength, and flexibility.

Mentally, beekeeping can have therapeutic effects. The act of caring for bees, observing their behaviors, and working in the garden can reduce stress and anxiety. The focus required for hive inspections and the meditative nature of beekeeping tasks promote mindfulness and mental clarity.

Encouraging Biodiversity

By creating a bee-friendly garden, you encourage biodiversity in your local area. Bees are attracted to a variety of flowering plants, and as they pollinate these plants, they help support a wide range of wildlife, from other pollinators to birds and small mammals.

A diverse garden not only benefits bees but also creates a balanced, healthy ecosystem. Planting a mix of native flowers, herbs, and vegetables ensures that bees have a continuous supply of nectar and pollen throughout the growing season, supporting their health and productivity.

Building a Legacy

Beekeeping can become a family tradition, passing down knowledge, skills, and appreciation for nature to future generations. By involving your family in beekeeping, you create lasting memories and instill values of environmental stewardship and sustainability.

Sharing the joys and challenges of beekeeping with children and grandchildren can foster a lifelong interest in nature and conservation. It's an opportunity to teach practical skills, responsibility, and the importance of working together to care for our environment.

Conclusion

Home beekeeping offers a wealth of benefits that extend far beyond the production of honey. It enriches your life personally, educationally, environmentally, and economically. By embracing beekeeping, you become part of a global movement to protect pollinators, promote biodiversity, and live more sustainably. Whether you're drawn to the meditative aspects, the educational opportunities, or the environmental impact, beekeeping provides a fulfilling and impactful hobby that can enhance your life and the world around you.

1.3 Overview of the Book

Welcome to the journey of beekeeping! This book, "Bee-Friendly: A Comprehensive Guide to Home Beekeeping," is designed to be your definitive resource, whether you are a complete beginner or someone with some experience looking to deepen your knowledge. Beekeeping is not only a fascinating hobby but also an essential practice for sustaining our ecosystems. Through this guide, we aim to equip you with the knowledge and skills necessary to manage your own hives successfully.

In this overview, we'll outline what you can expect from each chapter and how the book is structured to build your understanding and skills progressively. The book is divided into eight comprehensive chapters, each focusing on different aspects of beekeeping, from the basics of bee biology to advanced beekeeping techniques.

Chapter 1: Understanding Bees

In the first chapter, "Understanding Bees," we delve into the fascinating world of bees. We begin with the basics of bee biology, exploring the anatomy and lifecycle of bees. Understanding these fundamentals is crucial as it helps you comprehend the behavior and needs of your bees, ensuring you can provide them with the best care possible.

We also cover the different types of bees you might encounter, including honey bees, bumblebees, and solitary bees. Each type of bee has its unique characteristics and role in the ecosystem, and as a beekeeper, it's essential to recognize and understand these differences. Lastly, we explore the vital role of bees in pollination, explaining how they contribute to plant reproduction and the broader ecosystem.

Chapter 2: Getting Started with Beekeeping

"Getting Started with Beekeeping" is your step-by-step guide to setting up your first hive. This chapter helps you plan your apiary, including choosing the best location for your hives and understanding the legal considerations of beekeeping in your area. We discuss the essential beekeeping equipment you'll need, such as hives, protective gear, and various tools and accessories.

Additionally, this chapter guides you through the process of acquiring bees. You'll learn about different methods to obtain your first colony, whether purchasing bees, capturing a swarm, or getting a nucleus colony. By the end of this chapter, you'll be fully prepared to start your beekeeping journey.

Chapter 3: Setting Up Your Apiary

In "Setting Up Your Apiary," we focus on the practical aspects of preparing your hive and introducing bees to their new home. This chapter covers the assembly of hive components and the optimal placement of your hives to ensure the health and productivity of your bees.

You'll learn the techniques for installing package bees and introducing a nucleus colony to the hive. We also cover the essential aspects of feeding and caring for your bees, including different types of feed and feeding techniques. This chapter ensures you have a solid foundation to support your bees from the moment they arrive.

Chapter 4: Managing Your Hive

"Managing Your Hive" is a comprehensive guide to maintaining a healthy and productive bee colony. We discuss the importance of routine hive inspections, what to look for during these inspections, and how often they should be conducted. Monitoring the health of your bees is critical, so we provide detailed information on identifying common pests and diseases and how to manage them effectively.

Seasonal hive management is also a crucial aspect covered in this chapter. You'll learn about the different tasks and considerations for each season, ensuring your bees are well-cared for year-round. This chapter is designed to make hive management straightforward and effective, helping you maintain a thriving apiary.

Chapter 5: Honey Production

One of the most rewarding aspects of beekeeping is harvesting your own honey. In "Honey Production," we guide you through the entire process, from knowing when to harvest to the techniques for collecting honey. We cover the methods for extracting honey from the comb, filtering, and bottling it for use.

This chapter also explores the various uses for honey and beeswax, from culinary applications to craft and cosmetic uses. You'll discover the incredible versatility of the products you can harvest from your hives, making your beekeeping efforts even more rewarding.

Chapter 6: Expanding Your Apiary

As you gain experience and confidence in beekeeping, you may want to expand your apiary. "Expanding Your Apiary" covers advanced techniques such as splitting hives and raising queens. You'll learn when and why to split hives and the methods to do so successfully.

We also discuss the importance of a strong queen and various methods for raising new queens. Adding new hives to your apiary requires careful management, and this chapter provides the knowledge and skills you need to manage multiple hives effectively. By the end of this chapter, you'll be ready to grow your beekeeping operation confidently.

Chapter 7: Advanced Beekeeping Techniques

For those looking to take their beekeeping skills to the next level, "Advanced Beekeeping Techniques" covers specialized methods and innovative practices. We explore natural beekeeping, focusing on organic practices and sustainable methods that align with a holistic approach to beekeeping.

Migratory beekeeping is another advanced technique discussed in this chapter, highlighting its benefits and challenges. You'll learn about the best practices for moving your hives to follow seasonal blooms. Additionally, we introduce innovative hive designs, such as top-bar hives and Warre hives, providing options for beekeepers interested in exploring different hive structures.

Chapter 8: Troubleshooting and Problem-Solving

Despite your best efforts, you may encounter challenges in beekeeping. "Troubleshooting and Problem-Solving" is your go-to resource for addressing common beekeeping problems. We cover various issues related to hive health, environmental challenges, and pest management.

This chapter helps you identify threats to your bees and provides strategies for prevention and control. We also offer resources for beekeepers, including information on beekeeping associations and online communities where you can find support and advice. By the end of this chapter, you'll be equipped to handle any challenges that come your way.

Conclusion

In the "Conclusion," we reflect on the future of beekeeping and encourage you to continue your beekeeping journey. We emphasize the importance of ongoing learning and staying connected with the beekeeping community. Our final thoughts and encouragement aim to inspire you to maintain your commitment to beekeeping and to continue supporting the health of our planet through your efforts.

Appendices

The appendices provide additional valuable resources, including a glossary of beekeeping terms, a beekeeping calendar to help you plan your activities throughout the year, and useful contacts and resources for further information and support.

Index

An index is included to help you quickly find specific topics and information within the book, making it a practical and user-friendly resource.

CHAPTER I
Understanding Bees

1.1 Bee Biology

1.1 Anatomy of a Bee

Understanding the anatomy of a bee is crucial for any beekeeper, as it provides insights into their behavior, capabilities, and needs. Bees, like all insects, have a segmented body divided into three main parts: the head, thorax, and abdomen.

1.1.1 Head

The head of a bee is equipped with various sensory organs and structures essential for its survival and function within the colony. At the front of the head are the bee's compound eyes, which are made up of numerous hexagonal facets, allowing them to detect movement and perceive ultraviolet light. Bees also possess three simple eyes, or ocelli, located on the top of their head, which primarily aid in navigation and orientation during flight.

In addition to their eyes, bees have a pair of antennae that serve as highly sensitive organs for detecting odors and pheromones. These antennae play a crucial role in communication among colony members, as well as in locating food sources and identifying suitable nesting sites.

The mouthparts of a bee are adapted for both feeding and processing food. Bees have mandibles, or jaws, which they use to manipulate and collect pollen and propolis, as well as to build and maintain the hive structure. Their proboscis, a long, slender tube formed by the elongation of the lower lip, functions as a straw for sucking up nectar from flowers.

1.1.2 Thorax

The thorax is the middle section of a bee's body and serves as the powerhouse for its flight and locomotion. Attached to the thorax are three pairs of legs and two pairs of wings, which are essential for the bee's mobility and foraging activities.

The legs of a bee are equipped with specialized structures for pollen collection and transport. Each leg has a pollen basket, or corbicula, located on the outer surface of the hind leg. When visiting flowers, bees use their legs to gather pollen, which they moisten with nectar and pack into the pollen baskets for transport back to the hive.

The wings of a bee are membranous structures that are intricately veined for strength and flexibility. The forewings are larger than the hindwings and are connected to the thorax by a system of muscles that enable precise control over flight maneuvers. Bees are capable of flying at speeds of up to 15 miles per hour and can navigate complex aerial environments with remarkable agility.

1.1.3 Abdomen

The abdomen of a bee contains vital organs responsible for digestion, reproduction, and venom production. It also houses the wax glands, which secrete the beeswax used in constructing honeycomb cells.

One of the most distinctive features of a bee's abdomen is the stinger, a modified ovipositor found only in female bees. The stinger is a defensive weapon used to inject venom into threats such as predators or intruders. When a bee stings, the barbed stinger becomes lodged in the victim's skin, causing the bee to disembowel itself in the process, resulting in its death.

In addition to the stinger, the abdomen contains the digestive tract, including the crop, or honey stomach, where nectar is stored before being regurgitated and processed into honey. The abdomen also houses the reproductive organs, including the ovaries and spermatheca, which play a vital role in the queen bee's ability to lay eggs and maintain the colony's population.

Understanding the intricate anatomy of a bee provides valuable insights into its biology and behavior, allowing beekeepers to better care for their colonies and support the essential role that bees play in pollination and ecosystem health.

1.2 The Bee Lifecycle

Understanding the lifecycle of bees is fundamental for any beekeeper, as it provides insights into the various stages of development, behaviors, and needs of these remarkable insects. From egg to adult, each phase plays a crucial role not only in the life of an individual bee but also in the functioning of the entire colony.

Egg Stage

The lifecycle of a bee begins with the queen laying eggs. These eggs are tiny, almost microscopic, and are typically laid individually within the hexagonal cells of the honeycomb. The queen can control the fertilization of her eggs, laying fertilized eggs that develop into worker bees or unfertilized eggs that become drones.

Larval Stage

Once the egg hatches, it gives rise to a larva. The larval stage is characterized by rapid growth as the young bee consumes large amounts of food provided by nurse bees. During this stage, the larva molts several times, shedding its skin as it grows. The shape of the cell in which the egg is laid determines the size and shape of the resulting adult bee.

Pupal Stage

As the larva reaches full size, it undergoes a remarkable transformation into a pupa. During this stage, the larva is sealed within its cell by worker bees, where it undergoes metamorphosis. Inside the pupal case, the tissues, organs, and external features of the bee undergo significant restructuring, ultimately giving rise to the recognizable form of an adult bee.

Adult Stage

After a period of development, the adult bee emerges from its pupal case. Initially, it is soft and vulnerable, but it quickly hardens and darkens as it comes into contact with air. The newly emerged bee is often referred to as a "callow" bee and is ready to take on various roles within the colony. Depending on its sex and age, an adult bee will fulfill different duties, such as nursing, foraging, guarding, or mating.

Lifespan

The lifespan of a bee varies depending on its role within the colony. Worker bees, the majority of the colony, have the shortest lifespan, typically living for several weeks during the peak foraging season. Drones, or male bees, have a slightly longer lifespan, although they are expelled from the colony during times of scarcity. The queen bee, on the other hand, can live for several years, continuously laying eggs to maintain the colony's population.

Colony Dynamics

Understanding the lifecycle of individual bees is crucial for understanding the dynamics of the colony as a whole. The coordinated efforts of bees at different stages of development ensure the smooth functioning and survival of the colony. From the care of the brood to the collection of nectar and pollen, each bee plays a vital role in maintaining the health and productivity of the colony.

Environmental Factors

While the lifecycle of bees follows a general pattern, environmental factors such as temperature, humidity, and food availability can influence the timing and success of each stage. Changes in climate patterns, habitat loss, pesticide use, and disease outbreaks can also impact bee populations, highlighting the importance of conservation efforts and sustainable beekeeping practices.

Conclusion

The lifecycle of bees is a marvel of nature, with each stage finely tuned to ensure the survival and success of the colony. By understanding the intricacies of bee biology and behavior, beekeepers can better care for their colonies and contribute to the conservation of these vital pollinators. Whether for honey production, crop pollination, or simply the joy of observing these fascinating insects, the lifecycle of bees continues to inspire awe and wonder.

2. Types of Bees

2.1 Honey Bees

Honey bees, scientifically known as Apis mellifera, are perhaps the most well-known and widely recognized species of bee, largely due to their vital role in pollination and honey production. They belong to the genus Apis and are a subset of the family Apidae, which includes other important pollinators such as bumblebees and stingless bees. In this section, we will delve deeper into the fascinating world of honey bees, exploring their biology, behavior, and societal structure.

Biology of Honey Bees

Understanding the biology of honey bees is crucial for beekeepers and conservationists alike. These insects exhibit a complex social structure, with each individual playing a specific role within the colony.

Castes:

Honey bee colonies consist of three primary castes: the queen, workers, and drones.

1. Queen: The queen bee is the reproductive female in the colony. She is larger than the other bees and is responsible for laying eggs. A queen bee can lay up to 2,000 eggs per day during the peak season. Her pheromones regulate the behavior and harmony of the colony.

2. Workers: Worker bees are non-reproductive females that perform various tasks within the colony, such as nursing the brood, foraging for food, building and repairing the hive, and protecting the colony. They are the most numerous members of the colony.

3. Drones: Drones are the male bees whose primary function is to mate with a queen from another colony. They do not have stingers and are larger than worker bees. Drones are expelled from the hive during the winter months when resources are scarce.

Anatomy:

The anatomy of a honey bee is specialized for its role within the colony and its foraging activities. Key anatomical features include:

1. Proboscis: This elongated mouthpart enables honey bees to feed on nectar from flowers.

2. Compound Eyes: Honey bees have large compound eyes that provide them with excellent vision, particularly for detecting movement.

3. Antennae: The antennae of honey bees are highly sensitive and are used for detecting pheromones, communicating with other bees, and sensing environmental cues.

4. Wax Glands: Specialized glands on the abdomen of worker bees secrete wax, which is used to construct honeycomb cells for storing honey and raising brood.

Life Cycle of Honey Bees

The life cycle of a honey bee begins when an egg is laid by the queen. This egg hatches into a larva, which is fed by nurse bees until it pupates and emerges as an adult bee. Let's explore each stage in more detail:

1. Egg: The queen lays eggs individually within the cells of the honeycomb. Fertilized eggs develop into female bees (queens or workers), while unfertilized eggs develop into male bees (drones).

2. Larva: Once the egg hatches, it gives rise to a larva, which resembles a small, white worm. Nurse bees feed the larva a diet of royal jelly for the first few days, followed by a mixture of pollen and honey. Larvae molt several times as they grow.

3. Pupa: After the larval stage, the bee undergoes metamorphosis inside a capped cell. During this stage, the body of the bee undergoes significant changes, and it transitions into its adult form.

4. Adult Bee: The adult bee emerges from its cell and immediately assumes its role within the colony. Worker bees may live for several weeks during the active season, while drones typically have shorter lifespans.

Behavior and Communication

Honey bees exhibit sophisticated forms of communication and behavior that facilitate the smooth functioning of the colony.

Dance Language:

One of the most remarkable aspects of honey bee behavior is their dance language, which they use to communicate the location of food sources to other members of the colony. The most well-known dance is the waggle dance, performed by forager bees to indicate the direction and distance to a food source relative to the position of the sun.

Pheromones:

Honey bees produce a variety of pheromones that play crucial roles in colony cohesion, reproduction, and defense. For example, the queen bee emits a blend of pheromones that inhibit the development of ovaries in worker bees and maintain their loyalty to her.

Thermoregulation:

Honey bees engage in thermoregulatory behaviors to maintain the optimal temperature within the hive. During cold weather, they form a cluster around the brood to generate heat, while in hot weather, they fan their wings to promote airflow and cooling.

Economic and Ecological Importance

Honey bees play a vital role in both agricultural systems and natural ecosystems, making them indispensable to human well-being and biodiversity.

Pollination Services:

As pollinators, honey bees are responsible for pollinating a wide variety of crops, including fruits, vegetables, nuts, and oilseeds. Their role in agriculture is estimated to contribute billions of dollars to the global economy annually.

Honey Production:

Honey bees are also valued for their ability to produce honey, a nutritious and versatile food product. Beekeepers manage colonies for honey production, harvesting surplus honey while ensuring the health and welfare of the bees.

Biodiversity and Ecosystem Health:

In addition to their agricultural contributions, honey bees play a crucial role in maintaining biodiversity and ecosystem stability. By pollinating wild plants, they facilitate the reproduction of flowering plants and support diverse wildlife populations.

Conclusion

Honey bees are truly remarkable creatures, possessing complex social structures, sophisticated communication systems, and remarkable abilities that contribute to both human livelihoods and ecological balance. Understanding and appreciating the biology and behavior of honey bees is essential for promoting their conservation and sustainable management in an ever-changing world.

2.2 Bumblebees

Bumblebees, with their distinct fuzzy appearance and gentle buzzing flight, are among the most beloved and recognizable of all bee species. They belong to the genus Bombus and are known for their important role in pollination, as well as their unique behaviors and characteristics. In this section, we will delve into the fascinating world of bumblebees, exploring their biology, lifecycle, behavior, and their significance in both natural ecosystems and agriculture.

Bumblebee Biology:

Bumblebees, like other bee species, are members of the order Hymenoptera, which also includes ants and wasps. They are robust insects characterized by their large, hairy bodies and distinctive black and yellow coloration. Bumblebees have specialized structures that enable them to collect and transport pollen, such as dense hairs on their bodies known as setae and specialized structures on their legs called pollen baskets or corbiculae.

The Bumblebee Lifecycle:

The lifecycle of a bumblebee begins with the emergence of a new queen in late summer or early autumn. These queens have mated the previous year and have spent the winter hibernating in protected locations, such as underground burrows or leaf litter. In the spring, the queen emerges from hibernation and searches for a suitable nesting site, often underground or in abandoned rodent burrows.

Once a nesting site is established, the queen begins to lay eggs, which she incubates and cares for until they hatch into larvae. The queen feeds the larvae a mixture of pollen and nectar, which provides them with the necessary nutrients to grow and develop. As the larvae mature, they pupate and eventually emerge as adult worker bees.

Throughout the summer months, the colony grows in size as the queen continues to lay eggs and the worker bees forage for food. Towards the end of the summer, the colony produces new queens and male drones, which mate before the onset of winter. The old queen and male drones die off, while the newly mated queens hibernate and prepare to establish their own colonies in the following spring, thus completing the bumblebee lifecycle.

Behavioral Adaptations:

Bumblebees exhibit a range of fascinating behaviors and adaptations that contribute to their success as pollinators. One such adaptation is their ability to thermoregulate their body temperature, allowing them to forage in cooler conditions than other bee species. This is achieved through a process known as endothermy, whereby the bumblebee generates heat by vibrating its flight muscles while stationary, effectively warming its body.

Another notable behavior of bumblebees is their distinctive method of foraging known as "buzz pollination." Unlike honey bees, which primarily collect pollen by brushing it onto their bodies with specialized hairs, bumblebees actively vibrate their flight muscles while visiting flowers, causing the pollen to be released from the flower's anthers in a cloud of fine particles.

Ecological Importance:

Bumblebees play a crucial role in ecosystem functioning and plant reproduction through their pollination services. They are generalist foragers, meaning they visit a wide variety of flowering plants to collect pollen and nectar, making them effective pollinators for many plant species, including crops such as tomatoes, peppers, and blueberries.

In addition to their role in natural ecosystems, bumblebees also provide valuable pollination services to agricultural systems, contributing to the production of fruits, vegetables, and other crops. Their ability to forage in cooler temperatures and their effectiveness at pollinating certain plant species make them especially valuable pollinators in regions with temperate climates or in crops that require buzz pollination.

Conservation Challenges:

Despite their ecological and economic importance, bumblebee populations face numerous threats, including habitat loss, pesticide exposure, disease, and climate change. Habitat loss and fragmentation, resulting from urbanization, agricultural intensification, and land-use change, can restrict bumblebee access to food resources and nesting sites, leading to declines in population sizes and species diversity.

Pesticide exposure, particularly to neonicotinoids and other systemic insecticides, poses a significant risk to bumblebee health and survival. These chemicals can impair bumblebee navigation, foraging behavior, and reproduction, ultimately leading to colony collapse and population declines. Furthermore, bumblebees are susceptible to various diseases and parasites, such as Nosema bombi and the gut parasite Crithidia bombi, which can weaken colonies and make them more vulnerable to other stressors.

Climate change presents additional challenges for bumblebee populations, as rising temperatures, altered precipitation patterns, and shifts in flowering phenology can disrupt the synchrony between bumblebee foraging activity and the availability of floral resources. This can lead to mismatches between bumblebee populations and their food sources, reducing their reproductive success and overall fitness.

Conclusion:

In conclusion, bumblebees are fascinating creatures with unique biology, behaviors, and ecological significance. As important pollinators, they play a vital role in maintaining ecosystem health and biodiversity, as well as contributing to agricultural productivity and food security. However, bumblebee populations face numerous threats, including habitat loss, pesticide exposure, disease, and climate change, which require urgent conservation action to mitigate. By understanding the biology and ecology of bumblebees and implementing measures to protect and restore their habitats, we can ensure the continued survival and well-being of these essential pollinators for generations to come.

2.3 Solitary Bees

Solitary bees, as the name suggests, differ from their social counterparts in that they lead predominantly solitary lives. Unlike honey bees and bumblebees, which form colonies with complex social structures, solitary bees live and work alone. Despite their solitary nature, these bees play a crucial role in pollination and ecosystem health, often going unnoticed due to their less conspicuous lifestyle. In this section, we will delve into the fascinating world of solitary bees, exploring their behaviors, nesting habits, and contributions to the environment.

Behavior and Lifecycle

Solitary bees encompass a diverse range of species, each with its own unique behaviors and lifecycle patterns. While some solitary bees exhibit solitary foraging behaviors, others may exhibit a degree of sociality in nesting habits, forming loose aggregations in suitable nesting sites. However, unlike social bees, solitary bees do not have a division of labor within their nests.

The lifecycle of solitary bees typically begins with a mated female constructing and provisioning individual nest cells. Unlike honey bees, which maintain a perennial colony, solitary bees construct nests for a single brood cycle. The female solitary bee selects a suitable nesting site, which can vary depending on the species. Nesting sites may include abandoned beetle tunnels, hollow plant stems, or soil burrows.

Once a nesting site is selected, the female begins the meticulous process of constructing individual nest cells. She gathers materials such as mud, plant resins, or leaf fragments to construct partitions between cells. Each cell is provisioned with a mixture of pollen and nectar, which serves as food for the developing larva. The female then lays a single egg on top of the food mass before sealing the cell.

The development of solitary bee larvae within their nest cells varies depending on environmental conditions and species. Larvae undergo a series of molts as they feed and grow within their sealed cells. After completing their development, the mature larvae pupate within the cell before emerging as adults. Unlike social bees, where adults assist in nest maintenance and care for the brood, solitary bees rely solely on the provisions provided by the female during the larval stage.

Once emerged, adult solitary bees typically engage in solitary foraging activities, visiting flowers to collect pollen and nectar. They play a vital role in pollination as they transfer pollen from one flower to another while foraging. After completing their foraging activities, female solitary bees may seek out suitable nesting sites to construct nests for the next generation, thus completing the lifecycle.

Nesting Habits

Solitary bees exhibit a diverse array of nesting habits, with different species utilizing various nesting substrates and techniques. Understanding the nesting preferences of solitary bees is crucial for providing suitable habitat and promoting their populations. Some common nesting habits observed in solitary bees include:

Ground Nesting: Many solitary bee species are ground nesters, excavating tunnels in the soil to create nesting chambers. Ground-nesting solitary bees may prefer well-drained soils with sparse vegetation, where they can easily dig their nests. These bees often select sunny, south-facing slopes for nesting, where the soil warms quickly in the spring.

Cavity Nesting: Some solitary bee species are cavity nesters, utilizing pre-existing cavities or constructing nests in hollow plant stems, beetle tunnels, or other natural crevices. Cavity-nesting solitary bees may use various materials to partition nest cells within the cavity, such as mud, leaf fragments, or resin.

Wood-Nesting: Certain solitary bee species are specialized wood nesters, excavating tunnels in dead wood to create nesting chambers. These bees may prefer soft, decaying wood, where they can easily excavate nesting tunnels using their mandibles. Wood-nesting solitary bees play an essential role in forest ecosystems by aiding in the decomposition of dead wood and contributing to nutrient cycling.

Providing nesting habitat for solitary bees can be accomplished through various conservation practices, such as maintaining undisturbed areas with suitable nesting substrates, installing artificial nesting structures, and creating habitat enhancements in urban and agricultural landscapes.

Contributions to Ecosystems

Solitary bees play a crucial role in ecosystem health and functioning through their pollination services and interactions with flowering plants. While they may not be as well-known as honey bees or bumblebees, solitary bees are highly effective pollinators of a wide range of plant species, including many crops and wildflowers.

Due to their solitary nature and foraging behaviors, solitary bees exhibit distinct pollination behaviors compared to social bees. Solitary bees often exhibit a phenomenon known as "buzz pollination" or "sonication," where they use their flight muscles to vibrate flowers at specific frequencies. This vibration helps dislodge pollen from the flower's anthers, facilitating more efficient pollen collection.

The foraging behavior of solitary bees also contributes to the maintenance of plant diversity and ecosystem resilience. Unlike honey bees, which tend to focus on a few preferred floral resources, solitary bees may visit a diverse array of plant species for pollen and nectar. This broad foraging behavior increases the chances of cross-pollination between different plant species, promoting genetic diversity and enhancing ecosystem stability.

Furthermore, solitary bees are essential pollinators of early-flowering plants and crops, playing a crucial role in early-season pollination before the emergence of other pollinators. Their activity during cooler temperatures and inclement weather conditions makes them valuable pollinators in environments where other pollinators may be less active.

In agricultural landscapes, solitary bees contribute to crop pollination and yield production, complementing the services provided by honey bees and other managed pollinators. Incorporating conservation practices that support solitary bee populations, such as providing nesting habitat and minimizing pesticide exposure, can enhance pollination services and promote sustainable agriculture.

In conclusion, solitary bees represent a diverse and ecologically important group of pollinators that play a vital role in ecosystem functioning and food production. Understanding their behavior, nesting habits, and contributions to ecosystems is essential for conservation efforts aimed at protecting and promoting their populations in a rapidly changing world. By implementing habitat enhancements and conservation measures, we can ensure the continued health and resilience of solitary bee populations for future generations.

3. The Role of Bees in Pollination

3.1 How Bees Pollinate

Pollination is a crucial process in the life cycle of many plants, and bees play an essential role in this process. The intricate relationship between bees and flowering plants is a marvel of natural evolution, one that ensures the reproduction of plants and the survival of bees. To understand how bees pollinate, it is essential to delve into the behaviors, anatomy, and ecological interactions that facilitate this process.

The Process of Pollination:

Pollination occurs when pollen grains from the male anther of a flower are transferred to the female stigma. This can happen within the same flower, between flowers on the same plant, or between flowers of different plants of the same species. Bees, as pollinators, are integral to this transfer of pollen. Here's a detailed look at the steps involved in how bees accomplish pollination:

1. Attraction to Flowers:

Bees are attracted to flowers by various sensory cues, including color, scent, and nectar guides. Flowers have evolved to display vibrant colors and patterns visible to bees, who can see ultraviolet light, which humans cannot. This adaptation makes the flowers particularly appealing to bees. Additionally, the scent of a flower can attract bees from a distance, guiding them to the nectar-rich center.

2. Landing and Foraging:

When a bee lands on a flower, it begins foraging for nectar and pollen. Nectar is a primary source of energy for bees, while pollen provides proteins and other nutrients essential for their development. As the bee collects nectar, it brushes against the anthers, and pollen grains stick to the bee's body. Bees have specialized structures called scopae or corbiculae (pollen baskets) on their legs or bodies to gather and transport pollen.

3. Pollen Transfer:

As bees move from flower to flower in search of nectar, they inadvertently transfer pollen grains from one bloom to another. When a bee visits a flower, some of the pollen from the previous flower rubs off onto the stigma of the current flower. This pollen transfer is essential for the fertilization of many plants, leading to the production of seeds and fruit.

Bee Anatomy and Pollination:

The anatomy of bees is perfectly suited for pollination. Key anatomical features that aid in pollination include:

- Body Hair:

Bees are covered in tiny branched hairs that trap pollen grains electrostatically. When bees visit flowers, pollen sticks to these hairs and is then transferred to other flowers as bees continue their foraging.

- Proboscis:

The bee's long, tube-like tongue (proboscis) allows it to reach deep into flowers to access nectar, brushing against the anthers and stigmas in the process and facilitating pollen transfer.

- Pollen Baskets:

Many species of bees, particularly honeybees and bumblebees, have pollen baskets on their hind legs. These are used to store and transport pollen back to their hives. The act of collecting pollen into these baskets ensures that bees are effective pollinators as they transfer pollen from flower to flower.

Behavioral Adaptations:

Bees exhibit several behaviors that enhance their effectiveness as pollinators:

- Flower Constancy:

Bees typically exhibit flower constancy, meaning they prefer to visit the same type of flower during a foraging trip. This behavior increases the likelihood of cross-pollination between flowers of the same species, thereby enhancing reproductive success.

- Buzz Pollination:

Certain bees, such as bumblebees, engage in buzz pollination (sonication). They vibrate their flight muscles without flapping their wings, causing the flower to release pollen. This is particularly important for plants with poricidal anthers that release pollen only through small openings.

Ecological Interactions:

The interaction between bees and plants is mutualistic, meaning both parties benefit. Plants rely on bees for reproduction, while bees depend on plants for food. This interdependence has led to co-evolution, where the traits of bees and flowers have evolved together to enhance pollination efficiency.

Pollination Efficiency:

Bees are among the most efficient pollinators due to their behavior and anatomical adaptations. Compared to other pollinators like wind or water, bees ensure more precise and targeted pollen transfer. Their ability to visit numerous flowers in a single foraging trip increases the chances of successful pollination.

Factors Affecting Pollination:

Several factors can influence the effectiveness of bee pollination:

- Environmental Conditions:

Weather conditions such as temperature, humidity, and wind can affect bee activity and pollination. Bees are more active on warm, sunny days and less active in cold, rainy, or windy conditions.

- Habitat and Floral Diversity:

The availability of diverse and abundant floral resources in a habitat enhances bee foraging activity and, consequently, pollination. Monocultures or habitats with limited floral diversity may not support robust bee populations.

- Pesticides and Pollution:

Exposure to pesticides and environmental pollutants can harm bees, reducing their numbers and their ability to pollinate. It is crucial to manage pest control methods to minimize negative impacts on bees.

The Role of Bees in Agriculture:

In agricultural settings, bees are indispensable for the pollination of many crops. Approximately one-third of the food we consume relies on bee pollination, including fruits, vegetables, nuts, and seeds. Farmers often use managed bee colonies, such as honeybee hives, to enhance pollination and increase crop yields. The economic value of bee pollination in agriculture is immense, contributing billions of dollars annually to the global economy.

Conservation Efforts:

Given the critical role bees play in pollination and ecosystem health, conserving bee populations is of utmost importance. Efforts to protect and support bees include:

- Habitat Preservation:

Protecting and restoring natural habitats ensures that bees have access to diverse floral resources and nesting sites. Planting bee-friendly plants in gardens, parks, and urban areas can also support bee populations.

- Sustainable Agriculture:

Implementing sustainable farming practices that reduce pesticide use and promote biodiversity helps create a healthier environment for bees. Practices such as crop rotation, organic farming, and integrated pest management are beneficial.

- Research and Education:

Continued research on bee health, behavior, and ecology is vital for developing effective conservation strategies. Educating the public about the importance of bees and how to support them can also lead to positive change.

In conclusion, bees are extraordinary pollinators whose behaviors, anatomical features, and ecological interactions make them indispensable for the reproduction of many plants. Understanding how bees pollinate helps us appreciate their importance and underscores the need to protect and conserve these vital creatures for the health of our ecosystems and agriculture.

3.2 Importance for Ecosystems

Welcome

CHAPTER II
Getting Started with Beekeeping

1. Planning Your Apiary

1.1 Choosing a Location

Choosing the right location for your apiary is crucial for the success of your beekeeping venture. Bees are sensitive creatures, and their environment significantly impacts their health and productivity. Whether you're setting up a small backyard operation or a larger commercial apiary, thoughtful consideration of the following factors will help you select the optimal site for your bees.

Environmental Factors

Climate

The climate of your chosen location plays a vital role in beekeeping. Bees thrive in moderate climates with consistent temperatures and ample sunlight. While they can adapt to various conditions, extreme heat or cold can stress the colony and impact honey production. Research the climate patterns of your region and choose a location with moderate temperatures throughout the beekeeping season.

Floral Resources

A diverse range of flowering plants is essential for honeybees to forage and collect nectar and pollen. Look for areas abundant in flowering plants, trees, and shrubs that bloom at different times of the year. This ensures a steady supply of food for your bees and encourages colony growth and honey production. Additionally, consider planting bee-friendly flora in your apiary to supplement natural forage.

Water Source

Bees require a nearby water source for hydration and cooling the hive. Choose a location within flying distance of a clean and accessible water source, such as a pond, stream, or birdbath. Providing water near the apiary reduces the bees' need to travel long distances, improving their overall health and productivity.

Accessibility and Safety

Accessibility

Ensure easy access to your apiary for regular hive inspections, maintenance, and honey harvesting. A location with good vehicular access and proximity to your home or beekeeping facilities simplifies management tasks and reduces the time and effort required to care for your bees.

Land Ownership and Permissions

If you do not own the land where you plan to keep your bees, obtain permission from the landowner before setting up your apiary. This applies to both urban and rural settings. Additionally, familiarize yourself with any local ordinances or regulations related to beekeeping, such as hive placement, setback distances, and registration requirements.

Distance from Neighbors

Consider the proximity of your apiary to neighboring properties, especially homes, schools, and businesses. While honeybees are generally docile when foraging, their presence may cause concerns for individuals with allergies or phobias. Position hives in a location that minimizes interactions with neighboring properties and ensures the safety and comfort of both bees and humans.

Hive Placement

Sun Exposure

Place your hives in a location that receives ample sunlight throughout the day. Sun exposure helps regulate the temperature inside the hive, promotes brood development, and reduces moisture buildup, decreasing the risk of diseases such as chalkbrood and foulbrood. Orient the hive entrance to face the southeast or south to maximize exposure to the morning sun.

Wind Protection

While bees can tolerate some wind, excessive exposure to strong winds can stress the colony and disrupt their foraging activities. Choose a site sheltered from prevailing winds, such as behind a windbreak of trees, shrubs, or fences. This protects the hive from gusts and maintains a calm environment for the bees.

Hive Orientation

Position hives with the entrance facing away from prevailing winds and towards the morning sun. This orientation encourages efficient foraging and orientation flights while minimizing exposure to adverse weather conditions. Additionally, ensure adequate spacing between hives to prevent overcrowding and facilitate airflow for ventilation.

Conclusion

Selecting the right location for your apiary requires careful consideration of environmental factors, accessibility, safety, and hive placement. By choosing a suitable site that meets the needs of your bees and minimizes potential challenges, you set the foundation for a successful and sustainable beekeeping operation. Take the time to research and evaluate potential locations before establishing your apiary, and remember to monitor environmental conditions and hive health regularly to ensure the well-being of your bees.

1.2 Legal Considerations

When delving into the world of beekeeping, it's crucial to be aware of and abide by the legal considerations governing this practice. Regulations can vary significantly depending on your location, so it's essential to research and understand the specific laws and guidelines that apply to beekeeping in your area. In this section, we'll explore the typical legal considerations beekeepers encounter and how to ensure compliance while setting up and maintaining your apiary.

Understanding Local Regulations

Before embarking on your beekeeping journey, familiarize yourself with the local regulations governing beekeeping practices. These regulations may be established by municipal, county, or state authorities, and they can encompass various aspects of beekeeping, including hive placement, registration requirements, and zoning ordinances.

1. Hive Placement: Local regulations often dictate where you can place your beehives on your property. This may include minimum setback distances from property lines, neighboring residences, or public areas. Ensure that your hives comply with these setback requirements to avoid potential conflicts with neighbors and legal repercussions.

2. Registration and Permits: Some jurisdictions require beekeepers to register their apiaries or obtain permits before keeping bees. Registration helps authorities track bee populations and provides valuable information for disease management and pest control efforts. Be sure to inquire about any registration or permit requirements in your area and complete the necessary steps to ensure compliance.

3. Zoning Ordinances: Zoning regulations may restrict or regulate agricultural activities, including beekeeping, in certain areas. Verify whether your property is zoned for agricultural use and if any specific restrictions apply to beekeeping operations. Understanding zoning ordinances will help you avoid violations and potential fines.

Liability and Insurance

Beekeeping carries inherent risks, both for beekeepers and the surrounding community. As such, it's essential to consider liability issues and explore insurance options to protect yourself and your assets in the event of unforeseen incidents or accidents involving your bees.

1. Liability Concerns: Beekeepers may be held liable for injuries or damages resulting from bee stings or other bee-related incidents. Take precautions to mitigate risks, such as placing warning signs near your apiary and implementing safety measures to prevent bee aggression. Additionally, maintain your hives in good condition to minimize the likelihood of swarming or hive disturbances.

2. Insurance Coverage: Consider obtaining liability insurance tailored to beekeeping activities. This type of insurance can provide financial protection against claims or lawsuits arising from bee-related incidents. Consult with insurance providers knowledgeable about agricultural and beekeeping risks to assess your coverage needs and secure appropriate insurance policies.

Environmental Considerations

Beekeeping practices can have environmental implications, particularly concerning pesticide use, hive management, and bee forage sources. Being environmentally conscious and proactive in mitigating potential impacts is essential for promoting healthy bee populations and sustainable beekeeping practices.

1. Pesticide Awareness: Be mindful of pesticide applications in your vicinity, as certain pesticides can harm bees if they come into contact with treated plants or contaminated water sources. Stay informed about local pesticide use and communicate with neighboring landowners or agricultural producers to minimize pesticide exposure risks for your bees.

2. Forage Preservation: Preserve and enhance bee forage sources in your area to provide nutritious food for your bees and support local pollinator populations. Planting bee-friendly flowers, maintaining diverse vegetation, and avoiding the use of herbicides in forage areas can contribute to a thriving ecosystem for bees and other pollinators.

Conclusion

Navigating the legal landscape of beekeeping requires diligence, awareness, and a commitment to compliance. By understanding and adhering to local regulations, addressing liability concerns, and prioritizing environmental stewardship, you can establish and maintain a successful and responsible apiary. Remember to stay informed about evolving regulations and best practices to ensure the long-term sustainability and viability of your beekeeping endeavors.

With a solid understanding of legal considerations and a dedication to responsible beekeeping practices, you can embark on your beekeeping journey with confidence, knowing that you are contributing to the well-being of bees and the environment while enjoying the rewards of this fulfilling hobby.

2. Essential Beekeeping Equipment

2.1 Hives and Hive Components

Beekeeping, at its core, revolves around the hive. The hive serves as the home for the bees, providing them with shelter, security, and a place to store honey and raise brood. In this section, we will delve into the essential components of a beehive, exploring different hive types, their structures, and the importance of each component in the beekeeping process.

Hive Types

When it comes to choosing a hive type, beekeepers have several options, each with its own advantages and disadvantages. The most common hive types include Langstroth hives, top-bar hives, and Warre hives.

Langstroth Hives

Langstroth hives are the most widely used hives in commercial beekeeping due to their efficiency and versatility. They consist of rectangular boxes stacked vertically, with removable frames that hold the honeycomb. These frames allow for easy inspection and manipulation of the hive. Langstroth hives come in various sizes, including deep, medium, and shallow, depending on the beekeeper's preferences and the colony's needs.

One of the key features of Langstroth hives is their standardized frame size, which allows for interchangeability of frames and compatibility with various hive accessories. This standardization simplifies hive management and facilitates hive expansion or contraction as needed. Additionally, Langstroth hives can accommodate large colonies and are well-suited for honey production.

Top-Bar Hives

Top-bar hives are a popular choice among natural beekeepers and hobbyists who prefer a more hands-off approach to beekeeping. Unlike Langstroth hives, which use vertical frames, top-bar hives have horizontal bars from which the bees hang comb. The bars are spaced evenly across the top of the hive, forming a guide for the bees to build their comb downward.

Top-bar hives are prized for their simplicity and low cost of construction. They require minimal equipment and are easy to manage, making them ideal for beginners or beekeepers with limited space. However, top-bar hives may not be as efficient for honey production as Langstroth hives, and they may require more frequent inspections to prevent comb attachment and ensure proper hive health.

Warre Hives

Warre hives, also known as "vertical top-bar hives," are similar in concept to Langstroth hives but with some notable differences in design and management. Developed by French beekeeper Abbé Émile Warre in the early 20th century, Warre hives aim to mimic the natural nesting habits of honeybees more closely.

Warre hives consist of stacked boxes, similar to Langstroth hives, but with top-bars instead of frames. Each box serves as a separate "nadiring" or adding on from below. This nadiring method allows the bees to build their comb downwards, resembling the way they would construct comb in the wild.

Components of a Hive

Regardless of the hive type chosen, all beehives consist of several essential components that provide the bees with a suitable habitat and the beekeeper with the means to manage the colony effectively. These components include the hive body, frames or top bars, bottom board, inner cover, outer cover, and various hive accessories.

Hive Body

The hive body, also known as the brood chamber, serves as the primary living space for the bees. It houses the brood nest, where the queen lays her eggs, and provides storage space for pollen and honey. Depending on the hive type, the hive body may consist of one or more boxes stacked vertically or horizontally.

In Langstroth hives, the hive body typically comprises deep boxes, while top-bar and Warre hives may use shallower boxes. The size and configuration of the hive body can vary depending on factors such as colony size, climate, and beekeeping goals.

Frames or Top Bars

Frames or top bars provide structural support for the bees' comb and serve as a foundation for brood rearing and honey storage. In Langstroth hives, frames are rectangular structures that hang vertically within the hive body. They are usually made of wood or plastic and come with pre-installed wax foundation sheets to guide the bees in building straight comb.

Top bars, on the other hand, are wooden bars that span the width of the hive in top-bar and Warre hives. They provide a guide for the bees to attach their comb and are typically left bare or coated with beeswax for added reinforcement. Unlike frames, top bars allow the bees to build natural comb without the use of foundation.

Bottom Board

The bottom board, or hive stand, serves as the foundation of the hive, providing stability and elevation above the ground. It also serves as the entrance and exit point for the bees, allowing them to come and go freely while protecting the hive from predators and pests.

Bottom boards come in various designs, including solid bottom boards, screened bottom boards, and adjustable bottom boards. Solid bottom boards provide insulation and protection against drafts, while screened bottom boards aid in ventilation and pest control by allowing debris to fall through the screen.

Inner Cover

The inner cover is a removable lid that sits directly on top of the hive body, providing insulation and ventilation while preventing direct contact between the bees and the outer cover. It typically consists of a wooden or plastic frame covered with a layer of insulation, such as foam or felt.

Inner covers may include a feeding hole or notch for supplemental feeding and an inner cover shim for ventilation control. Some beekeepers also use inner covers with integrated bee escapes to facilitate bee removal during honey extraction.

Outer Cover

The outer cover, also known as the hive roof or telescoping cover, serves as the topmost layer of the hive, protecting it from the elements and providing additional insulation. It typically consists of a wooden or metal frame covered with a durable material, such as galvanized steel or aluminum.

Outer covers may come in various designs, including flat covers, gabled covers, and migratory covers. They are often topped with a metal or wooden cap to prevent water infiltration and secure the cover in place during inclement weather.

Hive Accessories

In addition to the essential components mentioned above, beekeepers may use various accessories to enhance hive functionality and productivity. These accessories include hive stands, entrance reducers, queen excluders, pollen traps, and hive wraps.

Hive stands elevate the hive off the ground, reducing the risk of moisture buildup and pest infestation. Entrance reducers help regulate hive ventilation and defend against intruders, while queen excluders prevent the queen from laying eggs in honey supers.

Pollen traps collect pollen from returning forager bees for human consumption or bee feed. Hive wraps provide insulation and weatherproofing during colder months, helping the bees maintain optimal hive temperature and humidity levels.

Conclusion

In conclusion, hives and hive components are fundamental aspects of beekeeping, providing bees with a suitable habitat and beekeepers with the tools to manage colonies effectively. Whether using Langstroth, top-bar, or Warre hives, beekeepers must understand the function and importance of each hive component to ensure the health and productivity of their colonies.

By selecting the appropriate hive type and components and maintaining them properly, beekeepers can create an optimal environment for their bees to thrive and produce honey and other hive products. Additionally, understanding hive anatomy and functionality enables beekeepers to monitor hive health, prevent disease, and address issues as they arise, ultimately contributing to the sustainability and success of their beekeeping

2.2 Protective Gear

In the fascinating world of beekeeping, one of the most critical aspects to consider is your safety. While bees are incredibly beneficial creatures, they can also become defensive if they feel threatened or if their hive is disturbed. This is where protective gear comes into play, serving as your shield against potential stings and ensuring that you can work confidently and comfortably around your bees. In this section, we will delve into the various types of protective gear available to beekeepers, their components, and how to choose the right gear for your needs.

Understanding the Importance of Protective Gear

Before we explore the specific types of protective gear, it's essential to understand why wearing protective clothing is crucial for beekeepers. Bees sting primarily in defense of their hive or when they perceive a threat to themselves or their colony. When you open a hive to inspect or harvest honey, you disrupt the bees' environment, which can trigger defensive behavior.

Protective gear serves as a barrier between you and the bees, reducing the likelihood of stings and minimizing their impact if they occur. Even experienced beekeepers who are accustomed to working with bees can benefit from wearing protective clothing to avoid unnecessary stings, which can cause discomfort, allergic reactions, or, in rare cases, more severe health complications.

Components of Protective Gear

Protective gear for beekeepers typically consists of several components designed to cover and protect different parts of the body. While the specific design and materials may vary depending on the manufacturer and personal preferences, the following are common components found in most beekeeping suits:

Beekeeping Suit:

The beekeeping suit is the foundation of your protective gear, providing full-body coverage to shield you from bee stings. It typically consists of a one-piece garment made from lightweight, breathable fabric such as cotton or polyester. The suit should be loose-fitting to allow air circulation while preventing bees from reaching your skin.

Veil:

The veil is a crucial component of beekeeping attire, protecting your face and neck from bee stings. It is usually attached to the beekeeping suit or worn separately as a hood that can be secured around your head with elastic bands or zippers. The veil is typically made from a fine mesh material that allows for clear visibility while preventing bees from accessing your face.

Gloves:

Beekeeping gloves are designed to cover and protect your hands and wrists, which are particularly vulnerable to bee stings during hive inspections or honey extraction. They are typically made from leather or synthetic materials and come in various lengths, from wrist-length to elbow-length, providing flexibility and dexterity while ensuring adequate protection.

Boots:

Footwear is another essential component of beekeeping protective gear, as bees can crawl up pant legs or find their way into shoes if not adequately covered. Beekeeping boots are typically made from durable materials such as rubber or leather and are designed to be worn over your regular shoes or boots. They provide full coverage up to the calf or knee, ensuring that your lower legs and feet remain protected.

Optional Accessories:

In addition to the essential components mentioned above, beekeepers may choose to wear additional accessories for added protection and comfort. These may include:

- Beekeeping jacket: Similar to a beekeeping suit but without the attached pants, providing upper body coverage.

- Beekeeping hat: An alternative to the veil, providing protection for the head and neck.

- Beekeeping sleeves: Separate sleeves that can be worn with a short-sleeved shirt to provide additional arm protection.

- Beekeeping socks: Socks specifically designed to be worn over pants or boots to prevent bees from accessing your ankles.

While these accessories are not essential, they can offer added protection in specific situations or personal preferences.

Choosing the Right Protective Gear

When selecting protective gear for beekeeping, several factors should be considered to ensure that you choose the right equipment for your needs:

Fit and Comfort:

The protective gear should fit comfortably without being too tight or too loose, allowing for ease of movement and airflow while providing adequate coverage. Ensure that the suit, veil, gloves, and boots are the correct size for your body to prevent bees from finding gaps or openings to access your skin.

Material and Durability:

Choose protective gear made from high-quality materials that are durable, breathable, and easy to clean. Look for suits and veils made from lightweight, tear-resistant fabric and gloves and boots made from sturdy materials that can withstand bee stings and regular use without compromising protection.

Visibility and Ventilation:

Opt for gear that offers clear visibility and adequate ventilation to prevent discomfort and fogging during hive inspections. Ensure that the veil has a fine mesh that allows for unobstructed vision while providing protection, and look for suits with ventilation panels or mesh inserts to promote airflow.

Budget and Value:

Consider your budget when purchasing protective gear, but prioritize quality and functionality over price alone. Investing in high-quality gear may initially cost more but can provide better protection and durability in the long run, ultimately offering better value for your money.

Maintaining and Caring for Protective Gear

Proper maintenance and care are essential to ensure that your protective gear remains effective and durable over time. Follow these tips to keep your beekeeping attire in top condition:

- Regularly inspect your gear for signs of wear and tear, such as holes, tears, or loose seams, and repair or replace any damaged components promptly.

- Clean your protective gear regularly according to the manufacturer's instructions to remove dirt, debris, and propolis buildup, which can compromise protection and comfort.

- Store your gear in a cool, dry place away from direct sunlight and moisture to prevent damage and mold growth.

- Avoid exposing your gear to harsh chemicals or solvents that may degrade the fabric or compromise its protective properties.

By investing in quality protective gear and maintaining it properly, you can ensure your safety and comfort while tending to your bees.

Conclusion

Protective gear is an indispensable component of beekeeping equipment, providing essential protection against bee stings and ensuring the safety and comfort of beekeepers during hive inspections and honey harvesting. By understanding the importance of protective gear, familiarizing yourself with its components, and choosing the right equipment for your needs, you can work confidently and safely with your bees, enjoying all the rewards that beekeeping has to offer. Remember to prioritize fit, comfort, and quality when selecting protective gear and to maintain it regularly to ensure its effectiveness and longevity. With the right gear and proper care, you can embark on your beekeeping journey with confidence and peace of mind.

2.3 Tools and Accessories

Tools and accessories are the backbone of successful beekeeping. While a well-maintained hive is crucial for the health of your bees, the tools you use play an equally important role in managing your apiary effectively. In this section, we'll delve into the essential tools and accessories every beekeeper needs to have on hand.

Smoker

The smoker is perhaps the most iconic tool in the beekeeper's arsenal. It consists of a metal canister with a bellows attached. Beekeepers use the smoker to generate smoke, which is then directed into the hive through the entrance or other openings. The smoke has a calming effect on the bees, making them less likely to become defensive or aggressive during hive inspections. Common fuels for smokers include pine needles, wood shavings, and dried leaves. It's essential to keep your smoker fueled and ready for use at all times.

Hive Tool

A hive tool is a multifunctional instrument designed specifically for beekeeping. It typically features a flat, sharp end for prying apart hive components and scraping off propolis and other debris. The opposite end may have a hook or blade for lifting frames or cutting away excess comb. Hive tools come in various shapes and sizes, but they are all essential for efficiently manipulating hive components without damaging them or injuring the bees.

Bee Brush

A bee brush is a soft-bristled brush used to gently remove bees from frames, hive boxes, or other surfaces without harming them. Bee brushes are indispensable during hive inspections and honey harvesting, allowing beekeepers to clear bees away from areas where they may be obstructing work. When using a bee brush, it's essential to handle it delicately to avoid injuring the bees or causing unnecessary agitation.

Feeder

Feeding your bees is sometimes necessary, especially during periods of nectar dearth or when establishing a new colony. Feeders come in various designs, including entrance feeders, frame feeders, and top feeders. Each type has its advantages and disadvantages, depending on factors such as climate, hive size, and feeding requirements. Regardless of the feeder type you choose, it's crucial to monitor the syrup levels regularly and refill them as needed to ensure that your bees have an adequate food supply.

Queen Excluder

A queen excluder is a metal or plastic grid placed between the brood chamber and honey supers to prevent the queen from laying eggs in the honey storage area. The excluder has openings large enough for worker bees to pass through but too small for the queen to fit. This ensures that the honey harvested from the supers remains free of brood and larvae, resulting in cleaner, more marketable honey. While some beekeepers choose not to use queen excluders, preferring to let the bees manage the hive's layout naturally, others find them indispensable for honey production and hive management.

Uncapping Tools

When harvesting honey, beekeepers need to remove the wax caps covering the honeycomb cells to release the honey. Uncapping tools come in various forms, including uncapping knives, electric uncapping knives, and uncapping forks. These tools allow beekeepers to cut through the wax caps cleanly and efficiently, minimizing damage to the comb and facilitating honey extraction. Proper uncapping is essential for maximizing honey yield and maintaining the integrity of the comb for future use.

Honey Extractor

A honey extractor is a mechanical device used to extract honey from honeycomb frames without destroying the comb. It consists of a drum or basket where the frames are placed and a hand crank or motor that spins the frames, causing the honey to be flung outwards by centrifugal force. Honey extractors come in various sizes and configurations, from small manual models suitable for hobbyist beekeepers to large motorized units used by commercial operations. Investing in a quality honey extractor can significantly streamline the honey harvesting process and improve the overall efficiency of your apiary.

Protective Clothing

While not technically tools, protective clothing is essential equipment for beekeepers, providing vital protection against bee stings and other hazards. A full beekeeping suit typically includes a jumpsuit or jacket with attached veil, gloves, and sometimes boots. The suit should be made of lightweight, breathable fabric that offers ample protection without impeding movement or causing discomfort. Additionally, wearing light-colored clothing can help deter bees from becoming agitated, as dark colors may trigger defensive behavior.

Conclusion

As you embark on your beekeeping journey, having the right tools and accessories at your disposal is essential for success. From smokers and hive tools to honey extractors and protective clothing, each item plays a crucial role in maintaining healthy colonies and maximizing honey production. By investing in quality equipment and familiarizing yourself with its proper use, you'll be well-equipped to manage your apiary with confidence and skill.

3. Acquiring Bees

3.1 Purchasing Bees

Purchasing bees is one of the most common methods of acquiring a colony for your beekeeping venture. It provides you with a ready-made population of bees, usually accompanied by a mated queen, already established in a hive. While it may seem straightforward, there are several factors to consider when purchasing bees to ensure you start off on the right foot.

Understanding Bee Packages and Nucs

When you decide to purchase bees, you will likely come across two main options: bee packages and nucleus colonies (nucs). Understanding the difference between these two options is crucial in making an informed decision.

Bee Packages:

A bee package typically consists of a screened box containing a specified number of worker bees and a separate queen in a queen cage. These bees are usually shaken from various colonies and combined to form a new colony. Bee packages are commonly available for purchase in the spring and are often favored by beginners due to their lower initial cost compared to nucs.

Nucleus Colonies (Nucs):

A nucleus colony, or nuc, is a small, established colony of bees housed in a smaller hive box. Nucs typically include frames containing brood in various stages of development, a laying queen, worker bees, and sufficient food stores. Unlike bee packages, nucs offer a head start as they already have a mated and actively laying queen, making them a popular choice for beekeepers looking to establish colonies quickly.

Factors to Consider When Purchasing Bees

When purchasing bees, several factors should influence your decision to ensure you receive healthy and productive colonies.

1. Source Reputation:

- Research the reputation of the bee supplier or breeder before making a purchase. Look for reviews and testimonials from other beekeepers to gauge the quality of bees and customer satisfaction.

- Consider purchasing bees from local sources whenever possible, as they are often better adapted to your region's climate and environmental conditions.

2. Bee Health and Genetics:

- Inspect the health and vitality of the bees before finalizing your purchase. Look for signs of disease, such as deformed wings or abnormal behavior.

- Inquire about the genetics of the bees, including their breed and lineage. Bees bred for desirable traits, such as honey production, gentleness, and resistance to pests and diseases, are preferred for beekeeping.

3. Timing:

- Plan your bee purchase according to the local climate and flowering seasons. Spring is typically the best time to introduce new colonies, as it allows bees to build up their populations and forage on abundant nectar and pollen resources.

4. Queen Quality:

- Evaluate the quality of the queen bee accompanying the colony. A well-mated and healthy queen is essential for colony productivity and longevity.

- Look for signs of queen vitality, such as a strong brood pattern, prolific egg-laying, and a calm demeanor.

5. Transportation and Handling:

- Ensure proper transportation and handling of bees to minimize stress and potential damage during transit. Bee packages and nucs should be securely packaged and ventilated to prevent overheating.

- Coordinate with the supplier to arrange for timely pickup or delivery to minimize the time bees spend in transit.

Conclusion

Purchasing bees is an exciting step in starting your beekeeping journey. By carefully considering factors such as source reputation, bee health and genetics, timing, queen quality, and transportation, you can ensure that you acquire healthy and productive colonies for your apiary. Whether you opt for bee packages or nucs, investing in high-quality bees will set the foundation for successful beekeeping and a thriving hive.

3.2 Capturing a Swarm

Capturing a swarm is one of the most exciting and rewarding methods of acquiring bees for your apiary. Swarms are a natural part of the honeybee lifecycle and can be a cost-effective way to start or expand your beekeeping operation. This section will guide you through the process, from understanding why swarms occur to safely and successfully capturing and installing them in your hive.

Understanding Swarming

Swarming is a natural reproductive process for honeybee colonies. It typically occurs in late spring to early summer when a colony becomes overcrowded. The old queen and about half of the worker bees leave the original hive to find a new home, creating a swarm. This process not only helps propagate the species but also ensures the health and vigor of bee populations.

Why Do Bees Swarm?

Bees swarm for several reasons:

1. Overcrowding: When the hive becomes too crowded, bees need more space. The congestion inside the hive prompts the bees to swarm.

2. Resource Availability: Abundant nectar and pollen can trigger swarming as it leads to rapid colony growth.

3. Old Queen: An aging queen's pheromones might not be strong enough to suppress the worker bees' urge to create new queens, leading to swarming.

4. Genetics: Some bee strains have a higher tendency to swarm than others.

Identifying a Swarm

A swarm is usually a large cluster of bees hanging from a tree branch, fence post, or other structure. It can appear intimidating, but swarming bees are generally docile since they are not defending a hive. Swarms can vary in size, from a few thousand bees to tens of thousands.

Equipment for Swarm Capture

To capture a swarm, you'll need the following equipment:

1. Protective Gear: A beekeeping suit or jacket, gloves, and a veil are essential for protection.

2. Bee Box or Swarm Catching Box: A portable container to hold the swarm temporarily. This can be a nucleus box or a ventilated cardboard box.

3. Bee Brush or Feather: To gently coax the bees into the box.

4. Pruners: To cut any branches or vegetation if the swarm is not easily accessible.

5. Ladder: If the swarm is high up, a sturdy ladder will be necessary.

6. Spray Bottle: Filled with sugar water to lightly spray the bees, making them more docile and easier to handle.

Steps to Capture a Swarm

1. Preparation:

   - Before you attempt to capture a swarm, ensure you have all your equipment ready. Time is of the essence, as swarms can move quickly to a new location.

   - Wear your protective gear and approach the swarm calmly. Bees in a swarm are generally not aggressive, but it's best to be cautious.

2. Assess the Situation:

   - Determine the swarm's location and accessibility. If it is on private property, obtain permission from the owner.

   - Check for any obstacles or hazards that might complicate the capture process.

3. Capturing the Swarm:

   - Place your bee box or swarm catching box as close to the swarm as possible.

   - If the swarm is on a branch, gently shake or brush the bees into the box. If shaking, do so firmly but gently, ensuring the majority of the bees fall into the container.

- If the swarm is on a structure, use your bee brush or feather to gently guide the bees into the box.

- Spray the bees lightly with sugar water to keep them calm and make them less likely to fly away.

4. Securing the Queen:

- The success of capturing the swarm largely depends on capturing the queen. Once she is in the box, the other bees will follow her pheromones.

- Watch for a large cluster of bees fanning their wings at the entrance of the box; this behavior indicates that the queen is inside.

5. Transporting the Swarm:

- Once the majority of the bees are in the box, close it securely, leaving a small ventilation gap.

- Transport the box to your apiary quickly but carefully, keeping it in a shaded, cool place during transit.

6. Installing the Swarm:

- Prepare the hive where you plan to install the swarm. Ensure it has frames with foundation or drawn comb.

- Place the box with the swarm next to the hive and gently shake the bees into the hive. If the queen is inside the hive, the rest of the swarm will follow.

- Close the hive and leave the entrance open to allow the bees to orient themselves to their new home.

Post-Capture Care

After installing the swarm, there are several steps you need to take to ensure the bees settle in and thrive:

1. Feeding:

- Provide the bees with sugar water (1:1 ratio of sugar to water) to help them build up their resources. Newly captured swarms need plenty of food to start drawing comb and establishing their new hive.

2. Monitoring:

- Check the hive regularly over the next few weeks to ensure the bees are adapting well. Look for signs of brood (eggs, larvae, and pupae) which indicate that the queen is laying.

3. Pest Management:

- Monitor for pests and diseases. Treat for mites if necessary and ensure the hive is healthy.

4. Integration:

- If you have other hives, keep an eye on the new colony's behavior and integration. Sometimes swarms can be more defensive, so observe how they interact with other colonies and manage accordingly.

Ethical Considerations

While capturing swarms can be beneficial for beekeepers, it's important to do so ethically:

- *Permission:* Always get permission before capturing a swarm on someone else's property.

- *Safety:* Ensure the safety of both the bees and people nearby during the capture process.

- Respect Nature: Only capture swarms that are accessible and safe to handle. If a swarm is in a hazardous location, it might be best to contact professional beekeepers or pest control services.

Advantages of Capturing a Swarm

1. Cost-Effective: Capturing a swarm is free compared to purchasing bees.

2. Genetic Diversity: Swarms can introduce new genetic material to your apiary, potentially increasing disease resistance and vigor.

3. Satisfaction: Successfully capturing and establishing a swarm can be incredibly rewarding and boost your confidence as a beekeeper.

Potential Challenges

1. Unknown Health Status: Swarms might carry diseases or pests, so it's important to monitor their health closely.

2. Acceptance Issues: The captured swarm may not always accept the new hive immediately, leading to absconding.

3. Time Sensitivity: Swarms can be unpredictable and may move on if not captured promptly.

Conclusion

Capturing a swarm is a thrilling aspect of beekeeping that allows you to expand your apiary in an economical and environmentally friendly way. By understanding the reasons behind swarming, properly preparing your equipment, and following ethical practices, you can successfully capture and integrate swarms into your beekeeping operation. Always remember to prioritize the health and safety of both the bees and those involved in the process. With practice and patience, swarm capturing can become a valuable skill in your beekeeping repertoire.

3.3 Installing Bees in the Hive

Installing bees in a hive is a critical step in starting your beekeeping journey. This process involves transferring your newly acquired bees into their new home, ensuring they are comfortable, safe, and ready to begin their work. This section will guide you through the steps of installing packaged bees, nucs (nucleus colonies), and swarms into a hive, providing detailed instructions and tips to ensure a successful start.

Preparing for Installation

Before you bring your bees home, it's crucial to have everything prepared. Make sure your hive is set up and ready, including all necessary components such as frames, foundation, and feeders. Here's a checklist to ensure you are fully prepared:

1. Hive Setup: Ensure the hive components are properly assembled and placed in the chosen location. The hive should be stable, level, and secure from predators and adverse weather conditions.

2. Feeder Preparation: Depending on the season and local forage availability, you may need to provide supplemental feeding. Have sugar syrup (a 1:1 ratio of sugar to water) ready for the bees.

3. Protective Gear: Wear your protective clothing, including a bee suit, gloves, and a veil. This will help you handle the bees safely and confidently.

4. Bee Transport: If you are transporting packaged bees, nucs, or a swarm, ensure they are secured in a cool, ventilated space during transit. Minimize jostling and temperature extremes.

Installing Packaged Bees

Packaged bees are a common way to start a new hive. A package typically contains several thousand bees and a queen in a separate cage. Here's how to install them:

1. Calm the Bees: Lightly spray the outside of the package with sugar syrup. This calms the bees and provides them with a little nourishment.

2. Open the Package: Carefully open the package. Remove the can of sugar syrup from the center, revealing the queen cage.

3. Inspect the Queen: Check to ensure the queen is alive and healthy. She should be active and moving around within her cage.

4. Place the Queen Cage: Suspend the queen cage in the center of the hive, between two frames. The candy plug should be facing up, allowing the worker bees to release her over the next few days by eating through the candy.

5. Release the Bees: Shake the bees from the package into the hive. A gentle shake will help dislodge the bees and allow them to settle into their new home.

6. Close the Hive: Once the bees are inside, close the hive gently and place the inner cover and the outer cover. Ensure there is a feeder available if necessary.

Installing a Nucleus Colony (Nuc)

A nuc is a small, established colony with a laying queen, workers, brood, and some stored food. Installing a nuc is generally easier than installing packaged bees:

1. Transfer Frames: Carefully transfer each frame from the nuc box into the prepared hive. Ensure you maintain the same order and orientation to minimize disturbance to the brood and stored food.

2. Inspect the Queen: While transferring frames, look for the queen to ensure she is present and healthy. Handle frames gently to avoid damaging the brood or harming the queen.

3. Place Additional Frames: If your hive box has more frames than the nuc, add the remaining frames filled with foundation or drawn comb.

4. Close the Hive: Once all frames are transferred and the bees are settled, close the hive. Provide supplemental feeding if necessary, especially if forage is scarce.

Installing a Swarm

Capturing and installing a swarm is a rewarding way to start a hive. Here's how to do it:

1. Capture the Swarm: Use a box or bucket to gently collect the swarm. If the swarm is on a branch, you can shake or brush the bees into the container.

2. Prepare the Hive: Ensure the hive is ready and in place before bringing the swarm home. Open the hive to allow for easy installation.

3. Release the Swarm: Pour or shake the bees into the hive. Try to ensure the queen enters the hive with the swarm.

4. Monitor the Bees: After releasing the bees, observe their behavior. If they start fanning at the entrance, it's a good sign they are settling in and accepting the hive as their new home.

5. Close the Hive: Once the bees have mostly entered the hive, close it up gently. Provide a feeder if necessary to help them get established.

Post-Installation Care

After installing your bees, it's essential to monitor their progress and ensure they are adapting well to their new environment. Here's what to do:

1. Frequent Inspections: Conduct regular hive inspections in the first few weeks. Check for signs of queen activity, such as eggs and brood, to ensure she is laying.

2. Feed the Bees: Provide supplemental feeding as needed, especially if natural forage is limited. Sugar syrup and pollen patties can help the colony grow strong.

3. Monitor for Pests and Diseases: Keep an eye out for common pests and diseases. Early detection and intervention are crucial for maintaining a healthy hive.

4. Weather Protection: Ensure the hive is protected from extreme weather. Add insulation or windbreaks if necessary to keep the bees comfortable.

Troubleshooting Common Issues

New beekeepers may encounter several common issues when installing bees. Here are some potential problems and solutions:

1. Queen Not Released: If the queen is not released after a few days, you may need to manually release her. Be careful and gentle to avoid harming her.

2. Bees Not Settling: If the bees are not settling into the hive, they may be attracted to another location. Ensure the hive is in a suitable location and there are no strong odors or disturbances nearby.

3. Aggressive Bees: If the bees are unusually aggressive, there may be an issue with the queen or the colony's health. Consider requeening or seeking advice from an experienced beekeeper.

By following these guidelines, you can successfully install your bees and set the foundation for a thriving and productive hive. Patience, careful observation, and timely interventions are key to becoming a successful beekeeper. As your bees settle into their new home, they will begin their crucial work of pollination and honey production, contributing to the health of your garden and the surrounding ecosystem.

CHAPTER III
Setting Up Your Apiary

1. Preparing the Hive

1.1 Assembling Hive Components

Before introducing bees to their new home, it's essential to ensure that the hive is properly assembled and prepared. This not only makes the transition easier for the bees but also ensures their long-term health and productivity. The process of preparing the hive involves several crucial steps, each of which contributes to creating an ideal environment for your bees.

Assembling Hive Components

Assembling a hive is a foundational skill for any beekeeper. A well-constructed hive protects bees from the elements and predators while providing the space and structure they need to thrive. There are various types of hives, but the Langstroth hive is the most commonly used due to its practical design and ease of management. Below, we outline the step-by-step process for assembling the components of a Langstroth hive.

Materials and Tools Needed

Before starting, gather all necessary materials and tools:

- Hive components: bottom board, hive body (deep super), frames, foundation, inner cover, outer cover, and, optionally, a queen excluder.

- Nails or screws

- Hammer or screwdriver

- Wood glue (optional, for extra stability)

- Hive tool

- Paint (for exterior protection)

- Paintbrush

- Protective gear (gloves, goggles)

Step-by-Step Assembly

1. Bottom Board

The bottom board serves as the foundation of the hive, providing a solid base. There are two types: solid and screened. A screened bottom board improves ventilation and helps control pests like Varroa mites.

1. Inspect the Board: Ensure the bottom board is free of cracks and defects.

2. Attach the Runners: If using a screened bottom board, attach the runners on either side to allow for airflow. Secure with nails or screws.

3. Apply Wood Glue (Optional): For added stability, apply a thin layer of wood glue along the edges where the runners meet the board.

4. Secure the Screen (If applicable): Attach the screen using nails or staples, ensuring it's taut and secure.

2. Hive Bodies (Deep Supers)

Hive bodies, also known as deep supers, are where the brood and food stores are kept. These need to be sturdy and properly assembled to support the weight of bees and honey.

1. Lay Out the Components: Arrange the four wooden pieces of the hive body – two shorter end pieces (width) and two longer side pieces (length).

2. Check Joints: Ensure that the joints fit snugly together.

3. Apply Wood Glue (Optional): For a more secure assembly, apply wood glue to the joints.

4. Assemble the Box: Fit the pieces together to form a rectangular box. Make sure the edges are flush.

5. Nail or Screw the Pieces Together: Use nails or screws to secure the joints. Hammer or drive screws at each corner, ensuring the box is square.

6. Reinforce the Corners: Add extra nails or screws at the corners for additional strength.

3. Frames and Foundation

Frames hold the foundation, which is where bees build their comb. Properly assembled frames are crucial for hive health and productivity.

1. Assemble the Frames: Each frame consists of a top bar, bottom bar, and two side bars.

2. Check for Fit: Ensure all parts fit together snugly.

3. Apply Wood Glue (Optional): Apply a small amount of wood glue to the joints for added stability.

4. Nail or Staple the Parts Together: Secure the joints with nails or staples.

5. Install the Foundation: Insert the foundation into the frame. For wax foundation, embed it into the frame using a small embedding tool or by heating wires if the frame is wired. For plastic foundation, simply snap it into place.

4. Inner Cover and Outer Cover

The inner cover provides insulation and helps with ventilation, while the outer cover protects the hive from weather.

1. Inspect the Inner Cover: Ensure it is free from cracks and fits well over the hive body.

2. Position the Inner Cover: Place it on top of the uppermost hive body, ensuring it fits snugly.

3. Inspect the Outer Cover: Ensure the outer cover is intact and provides complete coverage.

4. Place the Outer Cover: Position the outer cover over the inner cover. If using a telescoping cover, ensure it extends over the edges of the hive body.

5. Queen Excluder (Optional)

A queen excluder is a metal or plastic grid that allows worker bees to pass through but restricts the queen's movement, preventing her from laying eggs in the honey supers.

1. Inspect the Queen Excluder: Ensure it is clean and free from damage.

2. Place the Excluder: Position it between the brood box and the honey super.

6. Final Inspection

1. Check for Stability: Ensure all components are securely fastened and the hive is stable.

2. Paint the Exterior: To protect the hive from weather, paint the exterior with non-toxic, exterior-grade paint. Avoid painting the interior as bees prefer untreated wood.

3. Allow Paint to Dry: Ensure the paint is completely dry before introducing bees.

By following these steps meticulously, you create a robust and inviting home for your bees. Proper assembly and preparation of the hive are critical for the health and productivity of the colony. With your hive ready, you can move on to the next steps of introducing bees and caring for your new apiary residents.

1.2 Hive Placement

Choosing the right location for your beehive is critical to the health and productivity of your bee colony. Proper hive placement can influence everything from hive temperature regulation to foraging efficiency and colony security. This section will guide you through the key considerations and best practices for placing your beehive.

1.2.1 Sunlight and Shade

Bees are ectothermic, meaning their body temperature is influenced by their environment. Therefore, placing the hive where it can receive adequate sunlight is crucial. Ideally, the hive should be positioned to receive early morning sunlight. This sunlight helps warm the hive, encouraging bees to start foraging earlier in the day. Morning sun exposure also helps evaporate any moisture that may have accumulated overnight, reducing the risk of mold and mildew.

However, too much direct sunlight, especially in the hotter parts of the day, can overheat the hive. In hotter climates, providing some afternoon shade is beneficial. You can achieve this by placing the hive near a tree or structure that offers partial shade in the afternoon or by using a shade cloth.

1.2.2 Wind Protection

While bees need airflow for ventilation and cooling, strong winds can stress the colony and cool the hive too much, especially in colder climates. Placing the hive in a location sheltered from strong winds can help maintain a stable internal hive temperature. Natural windbreaks like hedges, fences, or buildings can be very effective. If such features are not available, you might consider creating an artificial windbreak using materials like burlap or lattice fencing.

1.2.3 Proximity to Water

Bees need water to regulate the temperature of the hive and to dilute honey for feeding larvae. Ideally, you should place your hive within a few hundred feet of a clean, fresh water source. If no natural water source is available, you can provide a man-made source such as a shallow container filled with water and floating objects like sticks or pebbles for the bees to land on. Ensure this water source is reliable and does not dry up during hot weather.

1.2.4 Forage Availability

The surrounding environment's floral diversity and availability directly impact the productivity of your bee colony. Place your hive in an area where bees have access to a wide variety of flowers throughout the foraging season. This includes gardens, orchards, wildflower meadows, and even urban landscapes with plenty of flowering plants. Bees typically forage within a 2-3 mile radius of the hive, so consider the broader landscape as well.

1.2.5 Hive Accessibility

While the needs of the bees are paramount, you must also consider ease of access for yourself. Regular inspections, feeding, and harvesting honey require that you can comfortably reach your hive. Ensure there are clear paths to and around the hive, avoiding any obstacles like tall grass or dense shrubbery. Also, consider the weight of honey supers when full – they can be heavy and awkward to handle, so having easy access for lifting and transporting is important.

1.2.6 Legal Considerations and Safety

Before placing your hive, check local regulations and ordinances regarding beekeeping. Some areas have specific rules about hive placement, especially in urban or suburban environments. These regulations might dictate how close hives can be to property lines or public spaces and may require you to register your hives.

Additionally, consider the safety of both the bees and people. Place hives away from high-traffic areas where people and pets frequently walk. If possible, erect a barrier or fence to guide bees' flight paths upwards and out of human traffic areas. This minimizes the risk of bee-human encounters and makes your beekeeping operation more harmonious with neighbors.

1.2.7 Elevation and Hive Stand

Elevating the hive off the ground has several benefits. It helps prevent moisture from seeping into the hive, protects against some predators, and reduces exposure to pesticides and other ground-level chemicals. Use a sturdy hive stand or concrete blocks to elevate your hive at least 18 inches off the ground. Ensure the stand is level and stable to prevent the hive from tipping over.

1.2.8 Hive Orientation

Orienting the hive entrance in the right direction can optimize the bees' activity. A common recommendation is to face the entrance south or southeast. This orientation ensures that the hive entrance receives early morning sunlight, which can help warm the hive and encourage early foraging. In colder climates, a south-facing entrance maximizes sunlight exposure, while in hotter climates, you might need to balance sunlight with shade considerations.

1.2.9 Ground Surface and Vegetation

The ground surface around your hive should be kept clear of tall vegetation and debris. High grass and weeds can harbor pests and make hive inspections more difficult. Maintain a clear area around the hive by regularly mowing or trimming the vegetation. You might also consider placing a weed barrier or mulch around the hive to keep the area tidy and reduce weed growth.

1.2.10 Avoiding Hazards

Finally, be mindful of potential hazards when choosing your hive location. Avoid placing the hive near pesticide-treated areas, as these chemicals can be harmful to bees. Also, be cautious of areas with heavy foot traffic or where animals might disturb the hive. If you live in an area with bears or other large predators, additional measures like electric fencing might be necessary to protect your hive.

By carefully considering these factors, you can select an optimal location for your hive that promotes the health and productivity of your bee colony while also ensuring ease of management and safety. Once your hive is properly placed, you'll be well on your way to successful and sustainable beekeeping.

2. Introducing Bees to the Hive

Introducing bees to their new home is a crucial step in establishing a successful apiary. This process involves careful handling and understanding the behavior and needs of the bees. There are two primary methods for introducing bees to a hive: installing package bees and introducing a nucleus colony. In this section, we will delve into the details of installing package bees, providing a comprehensive guide to ensure a smooth transition for both the bees and the beekeeper.

2.1 Installing Package Bees

Package bees are a popular choice for both beginner and experienced beekeepers. A package typically consists of three to four pounds of bees (approximately 10,000 to 12,000 bees), a queen bee in a separate cage, and a can of sugar syrup to sustain the bees during transit. The following steps outline the process of installing package bees into a hive:

Preparation Before Installing Package Bees

Before the arrival of your package bees, it is essential to ensure that everything is ready for their installation. This preparation includes assembling the hive components, selecting an appropriate location for the hive, and having all necessary tools and protective gear at hand.

1. Assemble the Hive: Make sure your hive is fully assembled and in place. This includes setting up the bottom board, brood boxes, frames, and inner and outer covers. Ensure that the hive is clean and free of any debris.

2. Location: Choose a location for your hive that is sheltered from strong winds, has good sun exposure, and is easily accessible. The area should also have a nearby water source and abundant forage for the bees.

3. Tools and Equipment: Gather all necessary tools and equipment, such as a hive tool, smoker, bee brush, and protective clothing (bee suit, gloves, and veil). Having everything ready will make the installation process smoother and safer.

Step-by-Step Guide to Installing Package Bees

Step 1: Prepare the Sugar Syrup

Bees in transit are fed with sugar syrup to keep them nourished. Once the package arrives, it's essential to provide additional food to help them settle into their new home. Prepare a sugar syrup solution by mixing one part sugar with one part water (1:1 ratio). Heat the water until the sugar dissolves completely, then let it cool to room temperature. This syrup will be used to feed the bees during the initial days after installation.

Step 2: Mist the Bees with Water

Gently mist the outside of the package with water. This calms the bees and reduces their flight activity, making them easier to handle. Be cautious not to over-saturate the package, as this can cause the bees to become agitated.

Step 3: Open the Package

Remove the outer cover of the package to access the can of sugar syrup and the queen cage. Carefully take out the can of sugar syrup. This will create a small opening through which bees might start to come out, so be prepared to move quickly and calmly.

Step 4: Remove the Queen Cage

The queen bee is the heart of the colony, and her introduction to the hive is critical. The queen cage is usually attached to a central wooden strip within the package. Gently remove the queen cage, being careful not to harm the queen or the attendant bees inside the cage with her.

Step 5: Inspect the Queen

Check the queen to ensure she is alive and healthy. A healthy queen should be active and exhibit a good body condition. If the queen is dead or appears weak, contact your bee supplier immediately for a replacement.

Step 6: Install the Queen Cage

There are different methods for installing the queen cage, but a common approach is to hang the cage between two frames in the brood box. Ensure the candy end of the cage (the end with a candy plug) is accessible to the bees. The worker bees will chew through the candy plug over a few days, gradually releasing the queen into the hive. This slow release allows the bees to become accustomed to the queen's pheromones, increasing the chances of her acceptance.

Step 7: Shake the Bees into the Hive

Once the queen cage is secured, it's time to introduce the bees to their new home. Hold the package over the hive and give it a firm shake to dislodge the bees. Bees will pour out of the package and into the hive. Continue shaking until most of the bees have been transferred. Be gentle but firm, ensuring the majority of the bees are inside the hive.

Step 8: Place the Remaining Bees

After shaking most of the bees into the hive, there will likely be some bees remaining in the package. Place the package at the entrance of the hive, allowing the remaining bees to find their way into the hive on their own. Bees are naturally attracted to the scent of their colony and will join the others.

Step 9: Provide Sugar Syrup

Place a feeder filled with the prepared sugar syrup at the entrance or inside the hive. This supplemental feeding is crucial for the bees as they establish themselves and begin foraging. Continue feeding until the bees no longer show interest in the syrup, indicating they have found sufficient natural food sources.

Step 10: Close the Hive

Carefully close the hive, placing the inner cover and outer cover securely. Ensure there are no gaps or openings where bees can escape or pests can enter.

Step 11: Monitor the Hive

In the following days, regularly check the hive to ensure the bees are settling in well. Monitor the sugar syrup levels and refill as needed. After about a week, inspect the hive to see if the queen has been released and if she is laying eggs. Look for signs of comb building and brood production, which indicate a healthy and functioning colony.

Troubleshooting Common Issues

Despite careful preparation and execution, beekeepers may encounter challenges during the installation process. Here are some common issues and their solutions:

1. Queen Rejection: If the bees reject the queen, they may ball around her and try to kill her. This can happen if the bees are not accustomed to her pheromones. If you notice aggressive behavior towards the queen, consider using a push-in cage or reintroducing her after a few days.

2. Excessive Bee Deaths: It's normal to see some dead bees after transit, but excessive deaths can indicate a problem. Check for signs of disease or poor transportation conditions. Contact your supplier if you suspect a health issue.

3. Lack of Foraging Activity: If the bees are not actively foraging, ensure they have access to food and water sources. Observe the entrance for signs of bee traffic. If activity remains low, inspect the hive for any internal issues such as pests or disease.

4. Robbing Behavior: Robbing occurs when bees from other colonies invade the hive to steal honey. Reduce the hive entrance size to make it easier for your bees to defend their home. Installing an entrance reducer or robbing screen can help prevent this behavior.

Post-Installation Care

After successfully installing package bees, ongoing care is essential to ensure the colony thrives. Here are some key points to consider in the weeks following installation:

1. Regular Inspections: Conduct regular hive inspections to monitor the health and progress of the colony. Look for signs of disease, pests, and queen activity. Early detection of issues can prevent major problems down the line.

2. Continued Feeding: Continue providing sugar syrup until the bees are well-established and natural nectar sources are abundant. This helps the colony build up its strength and resources.

3. Comb Building: Encourage comb building by providing frames with foundation. This gives the bees a structure to build on and speeds up the development of the hive.

4. Pollen and Protein: Ensure the bees have access to pollen and protein sources, either through natural foraging or supplemental feeding. Protein is vital for brood rearing and overall colony health.

5. Monitor Queen Health: The queen is crucial for colony success. Monitor her health and egg-laying patterns. If the queen is not performing well, consider requeening to ensure the colony's productivity.

6. Pest Management: Be vigilant about pests such as Varroa mites, small hive beetles, and wax moths. Implement integrated pest management practices to keep these threats under control.

By following these steps and guidelines, beekeepers can successfully introduce package bees to a hive and set the foundation for a healthy and productive colony. Patience, observation, and proactive care are key to overcoming challenges and ensuring the well-being of the bees.

2.2 Introducing a Nucleus Colony

A nucleus colony, or nuc, is essentially a small, established hive. It typically consists of a queen, workers, drones, brood, and some honey stores, all contained within a few frames. Introducing a nuc to your hive can be a highly effective way to jumpstart your beekeeping efforts, as it comes with a functional, cohesive unit of bees that are already accustomed to working together.

Advantages of Using a Nucleus Colony

1. Ease of Transition: Because the nuc is an already established mini-colony, the bees are less stressed during the transition compared to package bees. They have a queen they're familiar with and established brood, which means they can start building out the hive immediately.

2. Rapid Development: Nucleus colonies tend to develop faster than package bees because they include brood at various stages. This head start allows the colony to grow quickly, especially if introduced early in the season.

3. Greater Initial Strength: A nuc typically comes with a healthy, laying queen and a good mix of bees of different ages, including foragers and nurse bees. This diversity helps in rapidly establishing a strong and balanced colony.

Steps to Introduce a Nucleus Colony

Introducing a nucleus colony involves a few specific steps to ensure the bees transition smoothly into their new home. Here's a detailed guide:

1. Preparation:

  - Hive Readiness: Ensure your hive is fully assembled and placed in the desired location. It should be clean and dry, with frames in place.

  - Safety Gear: Wear appropriate protective clothing, including a veil, gloves, and a bee suit to prevent stings.

2. Transferring the Nuc:

  - Calm the Bees: Lightly smoke the nuc to calm the bees. Use a smoker with gentle puffs of cool smoke at the entrance.

  - Open the Nuc: Carefully open the nuc box. Remove the top cover slowly to avoid crushing bees.

  - Inspect the Frames: One by one, gently remove each frame from the nuc box. Inspect for the presence of the queen, brood patterns, and any signs of disease or pests.

  - Transfer the Frames: Place each frame from the nuc into the prepared hive body in the same order they were in the nuc box. This helps maintain the colony's internal structure and organization.

- Spacing: Ensure that the frames are evenly spaced in the hive body. This is crucial for the bees to properly build out comb and maintain brood areas.

3. Adding Extra Frames:

- Fill the Hive: After transferring the nuc frames, add additional frames to fill the hive body. These extra frames should have foundation or be ready for the bees to draw out comb.

- Proper Arrangement: Arrange the frames so that the brood frames are centrally located with empty frames or frames with foundation on the outside. This arrangement encourages the bees to expand the brood nest and store honey and pollen efficiently.

4. Closing the Hive:

- Secure the Hive: Once all frames are in place, carefully place the inner cover and outer cover back on the hive.

- Entrance Reducer: Use an entrance reducer to control the size of the hive entrance. This helps the bees defend their new home from potential intruders and manage temperature and humidity within the hive.

5. Feeding the Colony:

- Initial Feeding: Provide the colony with supplemental feeding, especially if local nectar sources are scarce or if the colony was transferred during a dearth period. Use a sugar syrup mixture (1:1 ratio of sugar to water) in a feeder placed inside the hive or at the entrance.

- Pollen Substitute: Consider providing a pollen substitute to support brood rearing until the colony can gather sufficient natural pollen.

6. Monitoring and Support:

- Regular Inspections: Conduct regular hive inspections (about once a week) to monitor the colony's progress. Check for brood development, food stores, and signs of disease or pests.

- Queen Performance: Observe the queen's laying pattern. A healthy queen will lay eggs in a consistent pattern, with few empty cells within the brood area.

- Pest Management: Keep an eye out for pests like Varroa mites, hive beetles, and wax moths. Implement integrated pest management practices as needed.

Troubleshooting Common Issues

Despite careful planning and execution, issues can arise when introducing a nucleus colony. Here are some common problems and solutions:

1. Queen Acceptance:

  - Issue: The colony rejects the queen.

  - Solution: If the bees show aggression towards the queen, consider requeening with a new queen. Alternatively, you can use a queen introduction cage to gradually introduce her to the colony.

2. Brood Problems:

  - Issue: Spotty brood pattern or lack of brood.

  - Solution: This could indicate a failing queen or disease. Replace the queen if necessary and inspect for brood diseases like American foulbrood or European foulbrood.

3. Low Foraging Activity:

  - Issue: The colony is not collecting enough nectar or pollen.

  - Solution: Provide supplemental feeding and check if the hive location has adequate forage. Relocating the hive to a better area might be necessary.

4. Pest Infestation:

  - Issue: Presence of Varroa mites, hive beetles, or wax moths.

  - Solution: Implement appropriate pest control measures such as screened bottom boards for Varroa mites, traps for beetles, and regular inspections to remove wax moth larvae.

Seasonal Considerations

The time of year plays a significant role in the success of introducing a nucleus colony. Here's how to manage introductions during different seasons:

1. Spring:

  - Ideal Time: Spring is the best time to introduce a nucleus colony. The abundant forage and favorable weather conditions help the colony build up quickly.

  - Swarm Prevention: Monitor the hive closely to prevent swarming. Provide ample space by adding additional supers as the colony grows.

2. Summer:

  - Feeding: Ensure the colony has sufficient food if nectar flow decreases. Continue supplemental feeding if necessary.

  - Heat Management: Provide ventilation and consider shading the hive to help the bees manage heat.

3. Fall:

  - Winter Preparations: Focus on building up food stores for winter. Reduce the hive entrance to keep out cold drafts and pests.

- Health Check: Ensure the colony is healthy and has a strong queen going into winter. Treat for Varroa mites and other pests as needed.

4. Winter:

- Monitoring: Regularly monitor the hive for food stores and feed fondant or candy boards if necessary.

- Insulation: Provide insulation or windbreaks to protect the hive from extreme cold.

Introducing a nucleus colony is a rewarding and effective way to start or expand your beekeeping endeavors. With proper preparation, careful handling, and diligent monitoring, your new colony will thrive and contribute to the health and productivity of your apiary. Remember, the key to successful beekeeping lies in understanding and supporting the natural behaviors and needs of your bees. By doing so, you'll not only enjoy the benefits of a healthy hive but also contribute to the vital role bees play in our ecosystem.

3. Feeding and Caring for Your Bees

3.1 Types of Feed

Feeding and caring for your bees is one of the most crucial aspects of beekeeping. Proper nutrition is vital to maintain a healthy, productive colony, especially during times when natural forage is scarce. In this section, we will delve into the different types of feed available for bees and the best feeding techniques to ensure your bees thrive.

Feeding bees involves providing them with substitutes for the natural nectar and pollen they typically gather. There are several types of feed that beekeepers can use, each with its specific purpose and application. The main types of feed are sugar syrup, pollen substitutes, and supplemental vitamins and minerals.

3.1.1 Sugar Syrup

Sugar syrup is the most common type of feed used by beekeepers. It serves as a replacement for nectar, providing bees with the necessary carbohydrates for energy. The syrup can be made using different sugar-to-water ratios depending on the season and the bees' needs.

1:1 Sugar Syrup: This mixture consists of equal parts sugar and water by weight (e.g., 1 pound of sugar to 1 pound of water). This syrup is typically used in the spring and early summer to stimulate brood production and colony growth. The 1:1 ratio closely mimics the consistency of natural nectar, encouraging bees to consume it readily.

2:1 Sugar Syrup: This mixture is made with two parts sugar to one part water by weight (e.g., 2 pounds of sugar to 1 pound of water). It is commonly used in the late summer and fall to help bees build up their stores for winter. The higher sugar concentration allows bees to store the syrup more efficiently as it requires less evaporation to convert it into storable honey.

How to Prepare Sugar Syrup:

1. Measure the required amounts of sugar and water.

2. Heat the water to a near boil (but do not boil it completely).

3. Slowly add the sugar while stirring continuously until it is fully dissolved.

4. Allow the syrup to cool before feeding it to the bees.

Feeding Techniques for Sugar Syrup: There are various methods to feed sugar syrup to bees, including internal feeders, external feeders, and frame feeders. Each method has its advantages and disadvantages, which we will discuss in detail later in this section.

3.1.2 Pollen Substitutes

Pollen provides bees with the protein necessary for brood rearing and overall colony health. When natural pollen sources are insufficient, beekeepers can provide pollen substitutes to ensure the bees receive adequate protein. Pollen substitutes come in various forms, including patties, dry powder, and liquid.

Pollen Patties: These are pre-mixed, dough-like substances that can be placed directly into the hive. They are convenient and ensure that the bees have continuous access to protein. Pollen patties are particularly useful during early spring when natural pollen is scarce but brood production is increasing.

Dry Pollen Substitute: This form can be sprinkled at the entrance of the hive or in a feeding station. Bees will collect it and bring it into the hive. Dry pollen substitutes are less commonly used but can be effective if bees are actively foraging.

Liquid Pollen Substitute: These are typically mixed with sugar syrup and fed to the bees. They provide a combined source of carbohydrates and protein, making them useful during periods of both nectar and pollen dearth.

How to Use Pollen Substitutes:

1. Determine the colony's need for protein based on brood rearing activity and natural pollen availability.

2. Choose the appropriate form of pollen substitute.

3. Place patties directly on the top bars of the brood frames or use feeders for dry or liquid substitutes.

3.1.3 Supplemental Vitamins and Minerals

In addition to carbohydrates and protein, bees also require various vitamins and minerals for optimal health. Some beekeepers provide supplemental vitamins and minerals to ensure that their colonies receive all necessary nutrients. These supplements can be added to sugar syrup or pollen substitutes.

Common Supplements:

- Honey-B-Healthy: A popular supplement that contains essential oils and vitamins to promote bee health.

- Pro Health: Another supplement that provides a range of vitamins, minerals, and essential oils.

How to Use Supplements:

1. Follow the manufacturer's instructions for dosage and mixing.

2. Add the supplements to sugar syrup or pollen substitute as directed.

3. Monitor the colony's response and adjust as needed.

3.2 Feeding Techniques

Feeding techniques vary based on the type of feed and the needs of the colony. Here, we will discuss the most common feeding methods, including internal feeders, external feeders, and frame feeders.

3.2.1 Internal Feeders

Internal feeders are placed inside the hive, typically within the brood chamber or above it. These feeders have several advantages, including protection from robbing by other bees and easy access for the colony.

Types of Internal Feeders:

Top Feeders: These feeders sit on top of the brood chamber and have a large capacity. They are ideal for providing sugar syrup in large quantities. Top feeders usually have a reservoir and a screen or float to prevent bees from drowning.

Frame Feeders: These are designed to fit into the hive like a standard frame. They hold sugar syrup and are placed within the brood chamber. Frame feeders are effective but can take up valuable space that would otherwise be used for brood or honey storage.

Division Board Feeders: Similar to frame feeders, these fit into the hive but are typically narrower. They are used when space is at a premium, and can be used to feed both sugar syrup and pollen substitutes.

How to Use Internal Feeders:

1. Choose the appropriate type of feeder for your hive configuration.

2. Fill the feeder with sugar syrup or pollen substitute.

3. Place the feeder inside the hive, ensuring it is stable and secure.

4. Monitor the feed level and refill as necessary.

3.2.2 External Feeders

External feeders are placed outside the hive, usually at the entrance or nearby. They are easier to monitor and refill without disturbing the colony but are more susceptible to robbing by other bees and pests.

Types of External Feeders:

Entrance Feeders: These feeders attach to the entrance of the hive and provide a continuous supply of sugar syrup. They are convenient but can attract robbers and predators.

Jar Feeders: These consist of an inverted jar with small holes in the lid, allowing syrup to drip out slowly. They can be placed near the hive entrance or on top of the inner cover.

Bucket Feeders: Similar to jar feeders, bucket feeders are larger and can hold more syrup. They are placed on top of the hive and can feed multiple colonies simultaneously if positioned correctly.

How to Use External Feeders:

1. Fill the feeder with sugar syrup or pollen substitute.

2. Place the feeder at the hive entrance or on top of the hive.

3. Monitor the feed level and refill as necessary.

4. Take precautions to minimize robbing and predation.

3.2.3 Frame Feeders

Frame feeders are an effective way to feed bees inside the hive without taking up too much space. They are particularly useful for providing sugar syrup directly to the brood area.

Types of Frame Feeders:

Standard Frame Feeders: These are designed to fit into a standard hive frame slot. They hold sugar syrup and have a built-in float or screen to prevent bees from drowning.

Division Board Feeders: Narrower than standard frame feeders, they can be used in hives where space is limited.

How to Use Frame Feeders:

1. Fill the feeder with sugar syrup.

2. Place the feeder in the brood chamber, replacing a frame if necessary.

3. Ensure the feeder is secure and stable to prevent spills.

4. Monitor the feed level and refill as necessary.

Monitoring and Adjusting Feeding Practices

Regular monitoring of your bees and their feed consumption is essential to ensure they are receiving adequate nutrition. Here are some key points to consider:

1. Inspect the Hive: Regularly inspect the hive to assess the colony's condition and feed consumption. Look for signs of stress, such as low brood production or dwindling bee population, which may indicate a need for more feed.

2. Adjust Feeding Quantities: Based on your observations, adjust the quantity and type of feed provided. During times of high brood rearing, increase the protein supply. When natural nectar sources are scarce, increase the sugar syrup feed.

3. Seasonal Adjustments: Modify your feeding practices according to the season. Provide more sugar syrup in the fall to help bees build winter stores and more pollen substitutes in the spring to support brood rearing.

4. Monitor Weather Conditions: Adverse weather conditions, such as prolonged rain or drought, can impact natural forage availability. Be prepared to supplement feed during these periods to prevent starvation.

5. Evaluate Colony Health: Healthy colonies will have a steady population growth, active brood rearing, and ample stores of honey and pollen. If you notice any deviations, investigate and address potential issues, such as disease, pests, or insufficient feed.

By understanding the different types of feed available and the best techniques for providing them, you can ensure that your bees remain healthy and productive throughout the year. Proper feeding and care are fundamental to successful beekeeping and will contribute to the overall well-being of your apiary.

3.2 Feeding Techniques

Feeding bees effectively is crucial for maintaining a healthy and productive colony, especially during periods when natural food sources are scarce. Here, we will explore various feeding techniques, detailing the methods and materials used to ensure your bees are well-nourished throughout the year.

Sugar Syrup Feeding

Sugar syrup is one of the most common methods of feeding bees. It is particularly useful during the spring and fall, when natural nectar sources may be limited.

Preparation of Sugar Syrup

The concentration of sugar syrup varies depending on the season:

- Spring and Summer Feeding: Use a 1:1 ratio of sugar to water. This lighter syrup stimulates brood rearing and mimics natural nectar flow.

- Fall Feeding: Use a 2:1 ratio of sugar to water. This heavier syrup helps bees store enough food for winter.

Instructions for Preparing Sugar Syrup:

1. Measure the desired amount of granulated sugar.

2. Heat the same amount of water (for 1:1) or half the amount of water (for 2:1) until it is hot but not boiling.

3. Slowly add the sugar to the hot water, stirring continuously until fully dissolved.

4. Allow the syrup to cool to room temperature before feeding it to the bees.

Feeding Methods

There are several methods to deliver sugar syrup to your bees:

- Boardman (Entrance) Feeder: This feeder attaches to the entrance of the hive. It is easy to monitor but may attract robbing bees from other colonies.

- Internal Hive Top Feeder: Placed inside the hive, this feeder holds a larger quantity of syrup and reduces the risk of robbing.

- Frame Feeder: Installed in place of a frame within the brood box, this feeder integrates seamlessly into the hive but may drown some bees.

- Bucket Feeder: A plastic pail with small holes in the lid, inverted over the top bars of the frames. Bees access the syrup through the holes, reducing the risk of drowning.

Fondant Feeding

Fondant is a solid sugar feed, useful during the winter months when liquid feed might freeze or when the bees are clustered and cannot access syrup feeders.

Preparation of Fondant

To make fondant, you'll need granulated sugar, water, and a small amount of vinegar or citric acid to prevent crystallization.

Instructions for Preparing Fondant:

1. Mix 4 parts granulated sugar with 1 part water.

2. Heat the mixture over medium heat, stirring constantly.

3. Add a teaspoon of vinegar or citric acid per kilogram of sugar.

4. Boil until the mixture reaches the soft-ball stage (238°F or 114°C).

5. Pour the mixture into a mold or onto a parchment-lined baking sheet.

6. Allow it to cool and harden before breaking it into manageable pieces.

Feeding Fondant

Fondant can be placed directly on the top bars of the frames within the hive. Ensure it is easily accessible to the bees, especially during cold weather when they are less mobile. Fondant provides a concentrated energy source that bees can use without needing to break their cluster.

Pollen Patties

Pollen is essential for brood development, and during times when natural pollen is scarce, pollen patties can provide the necessary protein and nutrients.

Preparation of Pollen Patties

Commercial pollen patties are available, but you can also make your own using a mixture of pollen substitute and sugar syrup.

Instructions for Preparing Pollen Patties:

1. Mix pollen substitute powder with enough sugar syrup to form a dough-like consistency.

2. Divide the mixture into patty-sized portions.

3. Wrap each patty in wax paper or plastic wrap, leaving one side open for bees to access.

Feeding Pollen Patties

Place the pollen patties directly on the top bars of the brood frames. Ensure they are positioned close to the brood area where nurse bees can easily access and distribute the protein to developing larvae.

Supplemental Protein Feeding

In addition to pollen patties, supplemental protein powders can be mixed with sugar syrup or dry fed to support brood production and colony health.

Instructions for Dry Feeding Protein Supplements:

1. Choose a protein supplement formulated for bees.

2. Place the supplement in a shallow tray or feeder within the hive or apiary.

3. Monitor consumption and replenish as needed.

Timing and Frequency of Feeding

The timing and frequency of feeding depend on the needs of the colony and the availability of natural forage. Here are some general guidelines:

- Early Spring: Feed light sugar syrup (1:1) to stimulate brood rearing.

- Late Summer/Early Fall: Feed heavy sugar syrup (2:1) to build up winter stores.

- Winter: Provide fondant or dry sugar if the colony's stores are low.

- Throughout the Year: Offer pollen patties or protein supplements during pollen dearths.

Monitoring and Adjusting Feeding Practices

Regular hive inspections are essential to monitor the effectiveness of your feeding strategy. Check the following during inspections:

- Syrup Consumption: Ensure the bees are consuming the syrup. If not, they may have sufficient natural forage, or the syrup may be fermenting.

- Pollen Patty Usage: Observe how quickly pollen patties are consumed. Adjust the size and frequency based on demand.

- Bee Health: Healthy bees will actively take feed and exhibit vigorous brood rearing. Weak or declining consumption may indicate health issues or queen problems.

- Food Stores: Assess the amount of stored honey and pollen. Supplement as necessary to avoid starvation.

Avoiding Common Feeding Pitfalls

Effective feeding requires careful attention to avoid potential problems:

- Prevent Robbing: Minimize the risk of robbing by reducing the hive entrance size during feeding and avoiding spilling syrup around the hive.

- Avoid Contamination: Use clean equipment and fresh ingredients to prepare feed. Contaminated feed can introduce diseases.

- Monitor for Mold: Especially in pollen patties, mold can develop if patties are not consumed quickly. Remove moldy feed immediately.

- Adjust for Weather: In cold weather, avoid liquid feeds that can chill the bees. In hot weather, ensure syrup does not ferment or spoil.

3.2.8 Advanced Feeding Techniques

For beekeepers looking to refine their feeding practices, consider these advanced techniques:

- Probiotics: Adding probiotics to sugar syrup can support gut health and disease resistance in bees.

- Essential Oils: Some beekeepers add essential oils like lemongrass or spearmint to syrup to improve bee health and attractiveness of the feed.

- Varied Diet: Provide a variety of feed types to ensure a balanced diet, supporting overall colony health and productivity.

Sustainable Feeding Practices

Aim for sustainable feeding practices that reduce reliance on supplemental feeding by enhancing natural forage availability:

- Planting Bee-Friendly Flora: Grow a variety of nectar and pollen-rich plants to provide natural forage throughout the season.

- Habitat Enhancement: Maintain hedgerows, wildflower meadows, and other natural habitats to support diverse forage options.

- Seasonal Management: Align colony management practices with local bloom cycles to optimize natural feeding opportunities.

Conclusion

Feeding and caring for your bees is a dynamic and essential aspect of beekeeping. By understanding and implementing various feeding techniques, you can ensure the health and productivity of your colonies. Regular monitoring, adjusting feeding practices based on seasonal needs, and integrating sustainable approaches will contribute to a thriving apiary. Remember, a well-fed bee is a happy bee, and happy bees are the foundation of successful beekeeping.

CHAPTER IV
Managing Your Hive

1. Routine Hive Inspections

Routine hive inspections are a fundamental aspect of successful beekeeping. Regularly checking your hive helps you stay ahead of potential problems and ensure the overall health and productivity of your bee colony. Inspections allow you to monitor the well-being of your bees, assess the condition of the hive, and take proactive steps to maintain a healthy environment for your colony.

1.1 What to Look For

During routine inspections, beekeepers should focus on several key elements to assess the health and functionality of the hive. Here's a detailed breakdown of what to look for during a hive inspection:

1. Queen Status:

The queen is the heart of the hive, and her health and productivity are crucial for the colony's success. When inspecting the hive, look for the presence of the queen or signs that she is actively laying eggs. Key indicators include:

- Presence of the Queen: Spotting the queen herself can be challenging, especially in a large colony. She is usually larger than the worker bees, with a longer abdomen and a distinct, unmarked thorax. Marking the queen with a small dot of paint can make her easier to find.

- Eggs: Look for freshly laid eggs in the cells. Eggs stand upright on the bottom of the cell for the first three days before they hatch into larvae. The presence of eggs indicates that the queen has been laying recently.

- Brood Pattern: A healthy queen lays eggs in a consistent pattern, creating a solid brood pattern with few empty cells. This indicates her fertility and the overall health of the colony. Spotty brood patterns can be a sign of problems such as disease, pests, or a failing queen.

2. Brood Health:

Examine the brood carefully for signs of health issues. Healthy brood should appear uniform and free from irregularities. Specific things to look for include:

- Capped Brood: Check the capped brood cells to ensure they are evenly capped and have a slight dome shape. Sunken or perforated cappings can be signs of disease, such as American foulbrood.

- Larvae: Healthy larvae are pearly white and curled up at the bottom of the cells. Discolored or malformed larvae can indicate problems such as European foulbrood or other brood diseases.

- Pupae: If you see pupae, ensure they are developing properly. Any abnormalities, such as discolored or deformed pupae, should be investigated further.

3. Honey and Pollen Stores:

Adequate food stores are essential for the colony's survival, especially during times when foraging is not possible. During inspections, check for:

- Honey Stores: Ensure the hive has sufficient honey stores to sustain the colony. Honey is stored in the upper part of the frames and should be plentiful, particularly as the hive prepares for winter.

- Pollen Stores: Pollen is the primary protein source for bees and is vital for brood rearing. Look for cells filled with different colored pollen, typically stored near the brood area.

4. Hive Condition:

The physical condition of the hive is crucial for the protection and productivity of the colony. Inspect the hive components for any signs of wear or damage, including:

- Frames and Foundation: Check the frames for stability and ensure the foundation is properly drawn out. Damaged or old frames should be replaced.

- Hive Body: Inspect the hive body for cracks, gaps, or any signs of wear that could allow pests or moisture to enter. Ensure that the hive is structurally sound and provides a secure environment for the bees.

- Ventilation and Moisture Control: Proper ventilation is essential to prevent moisture buildup inside the hive, which can lead to mold and other issues. Ensure that the hive has adequate ventilation, particularly during the winter months.

5. Signs of Pests and Diseases:

Regularly monitoring for pests and diseases is critical to maintaining a healthy hive. During inspections, look for:

- Varroa Mites: These parasitic mites are a significant threat to bee colonies. Check for mites on bees, particularly on the drone brood, which is more susceptible to infestation. Using a screened bottom board or a mite board can help you monitor mite levels.

- Wax Moths: Look for signs of wax moth infestation, such as webbing or tunnels in the comb. Wax moths can cause significant damage to the hive, especially if left unchecked.

- Small Hive Beetles: Inspect the hive for small hive beetles, which can damage comb, stored honey, and pollen. Look for beetles hiding in cracks and crevices within the hive.

- Signs of Disease: Be vigilant for symptoms of common bee diseases, such as chalkbrood, nosema, or American and European foulbrood. Unusual smells, discolored or deformed bees, and irregular brood patterns can all be indicators of disease.

6. Colony Behavior:

Observing the behavior of the colony can provide insights into its overall health and well-being. During inspections, take note of:

- Temperament: Assess the bees' behavior during the inspection. A calm and gentle colony usually indicates good health, while overly aggressive or agitated behavior can signal underlying issues, such as queenlessness or disease.

- Foraging Activity: Healthy hives should have a steady flow of bees coming and going, indicating active foraging. Lack of foraging activity can be a sign of problems within the hive.

- Cleanliness: Bees are meticulous about keeping their hive clean. Excessive debris, dead bees, or other waste inside the hive can indicate issues with hive health or hygiene.

7. Space Management:

Proper space management is crucial to prevent overcrowding and swarming. During inspections, evaluate:

- Brood Space: Ensure that the queen has enough space to lay eggs. If the brood area is overcrowded, consider adding additional frames or a new hive body to provide more space.

- Honey Storage: Ensure there is adequate space for honey storage. If the hive is becoming congested with honey stores, consider adding supers to accommodate the excess.

8. Queen Cells:

Queen cells are special cells where new queens are reared. Their presence can indicate swarming or supersedure:

- Swarm Cells: These are usually found at the edges or bottom of the frames and indicate that the colony is preparing to swarm. Swarming is a natural process of colony reproduction but can lead to a significant reduction in the number of bees in your hive.

- Supersedure Cells: These are typically located in the middle of the frames and indicate that the colony is preparing to replace an old or failing queen. Supersedure is a natural process and usually results in a new queen taking over the colony.

9. Hive Entrance:

Observing the hive entrance can provide valuable insights without even opening the hive:

- Bee Activity: A healthy hive will have a steady stream of bees entering and exiting, carrying pollen and nectar. Watch for normal flight patterns and foraging behavior.

- Guard Bees: These bees defend the entrance against intruders. Observe their behavior to ensure they are actively protecting the hive.

- Dead Bees: While some dead bees outside the hive are normal, a large number can indicate problems such as poisoning, disease, or pest attacks.

10. Propolis and Wax Production:

Propolis and wax production are indicators of colony health and activity:

- Propolis: Bees use propolis to seal gaps and cracks in the hive. Healthy colonies typically produce a significant amount of propolis.

- Wax Production: Active wax production indicates a healthy, growing colony. New, white wax is a sign that the bees are busy building and expanding the hive.

Conclusion:

Routine hive inspections are an essential part of beekeeping, allowing you to monitor and manage the health and productivity of your colony effectively. By knowing what to look for during inspections, you can identify potential issues early and take the necessary steps to address them, ensuring a thriving and productive hive. Regular inspections help you stay in tune with your bees and provide the best possible care for your colony, leading to a successful and rewarding beekeeping experience.

1.2 Frequency of Inspections

Inspecting your beehive on a regular basis is crucial for maintaining the health and productivity of your colony. The frequency of these inspections can vary depending on the season, the specific needs of your hive, and the overall goals of your beekeeping operation. Here, we'll delve into the recommended frequency of hive inspections throughout the year, providing detailed guidance to help you establish an effective inspection schedule.

Spring Inspections

Spring is a period of rapid growth and activity in the hive. As the weather warms and flowers begin to bloom, your bees will become more active, and the queen will ramp up her egg-laying. This makes spring a critical time for inspections to ensure your hive is healthy and growing.

Early Spring (March to April):

1. Initial Spring Inspection: As soon as the weather permits and temperatures are consistently above 50°F (10°C), conduct your first thorough inspection. This initial inspection is crucial to assess the colony's health after winter and to check for signs of starvation, disease, or other issues. Look for the presence of the queen, brood pattern, and food stores.

2. Bi-weekly Inspections: During early spring, inspect your hive every two weeks. This allows you to monitor the queen's laying pattern, ensure that the colony is expanding, and prevent swarming. Pay close attention to the brood pattern and the presence of queen cells, which can indicate the hive's intention to swarm.

Late Spring (May to June):

1. Weekly Inspections: As the colony grows rapidly in late spring, increase the frequency of inspections to once a week. This helps in managing the hive's expansion, adding additional space as needed (such as adding supers), and preventing swarming. Look for signs of overcrowding and ensure there is ample space for the queen to lay eggs.

2. Swarm Prevention: Late spring is a peak swarming period. During inspections, look for swarm cells (large, peanut-shaped cells hanging from the bottom of frames) and take preventive measures if necessary, such as splitting the hive or removing queen cells.

Summer Inspections

Summer is a period of peak activity for your hive, with bees foraging extensively and the colony reaching its maximum size. Inspections during this time focus on maintaining hive health and managing honey production.

Early to Mid-Summer (July to August):

1. Bi-weekly Inspections: Conduct inspections every two weeks to monitor hive health and honey production. Check for signs of disease, pests, and adequate ventilation. Ensure that the bees have enough space for honey storage and consider adding more supers if needed.

2. Honey Harvesting: Depending on your region and the nectar flow, you may need to inspect and harvest honey. Be mindful of leaving enough honey for the bees to sustain themselves, especially if there is a dearth period.

Late Summer (August to September):

1. Monthly Inspections: As the nectar flow decreases, reduce the frequency of inspections to once a month. During these inspections, focus on assessing the overall health of the colony, monitoring for pests like Varroa mites, and ensuring the hive has adequate food stores for the upcoming winter.

2. Preparing for Fall: Begin preparing the hive for the fall and winter months. This includes checking and potentially treating for pests and diseases, ensuring there is enough food stored, and making any necessary repairs or adjustments to the hive structure.

Fall Inspections

Fall is a time of preparation for winter. The focus shifts to ensuring the colony is healthy and has enough resources to survive the colder months.

Early Fall (September to October):

1. Bi-weekly Inspections: In early fall, inspect your hive every two weeks. Check for the presence of the queen and assess the brood pattern to ensure the colony is strong heading into winter. Monitor food stores and continue to check for pests and diseases.

2. Feeding: If necessary, start supplemental feeding to ensure the colony has enough food for winter. This can include sugar syrup or fondant.

Late Fall (November):

1. Final Fall Inspection: Conduct a final thorough inspection before winter sets in. Ensure that the hive is well-ventilated and has sufficient food stores. Reduce the entrance size to prevent pests and to retain heat.

2. Winter Preparations: Make any final preparations for winter, such as insulating the hive, adding a moisture board, and ensuring there is adequate ventilation.

Winter Inspections

Winter is a challenging time for beekeeping, with limited opportunities for inspections. The goal during winter is to ensure the colony remains healthy and survives until spring.

Early Winter (December to January):

1. Minimal Disturbance: Limit inspections during the cold months to avoid disturbing the cluster and causing heat loss. Only inspect the hive if there are signs of distress, such as a lack of activity or unusual sounds.

2. External Checks: Regularly check the hive from the outside for any signs of damage, moisture buildup, or pest activity. Ensure the entrance is clear of snow and debris.

Late Winter (February):

1. Quick Checks: As temperatures begin to rise slightly, you can perform quick checks to ensure the colony is still alive and has enough food. Consider adding supplemental feeding if food stores are low.

2. Preparing for Spring: Begin planning for the upcoming spring inspections and any necessary maintenance or equipment purchases.

Conclusion

Regular hive inspections are a fundamental aspect of successful beekeeping. By adhering to a structured inspection schedule and adjusting the frequency based on seasonal needs, you can ensure the health and productivity of your colony. Remember, each hive is unique, and over time, you will develop a deeper understanding of your bees' specific needs and behaviors, allowing you to fine-tune your inspection routine accordingly.

2. Monitoring Bee Health

2.1 Identifying Common Pests

Bee health is paramount to the success of your hive. Just like any other living organism, bees are susceptible to various pests and diseases that can compromise their well-being and productivity. Identifying and addressing these issues promptly is crucial for maintaining a thriving colony. In this section, we will explore the common pests that can afflict honeybee colonies and discuss effective strategies for monitoring and managing their impact.

Identifying Common Pests

Maintaining a vigilant eye on your hive is essential for early detection and prevention of pest infestations. By familiarizing yourself with the signs and symptoms associated with common bee pests, you can take proactive measures to safeguard your colony's health. Let's delve into some of the most prevalent pests that beekeepers encounter:

Varroa Mites (Varroa destructor)

Varroa mites are arguably the most significant threat to honeybee colonies worldwide. These external parasites feed on both adult bees and developing brood, weakening the bees and transmitting viruses that can devastate entire hives. Identifying varroa mite infestations early is crucial for implementing effective control measures.

Signs of Varroa Infestation:

1. Visible Mites: Adult varroa mites can often be seen on the bodies of adult bees, particularly in the thoracic region.

2. Deformed Wings: Bees infested with varroa mites may exhibit deformed or misshapen wings, a telltale sign of viral infection transmitted by the mites.

3. Reduced Bee Population: A sudden decline in the number of adult bees in the hive, especially during the brood-rearing season, may indicate a severe varroa infestation.

4. Presence of Mite Frass: Varroa mites leave behind fecal deposits, known as "mite frass," on the comb surface, which can serve as a visual indicator of infestation.

Management Strategies:

1. Integrated Pest Management (IPM): Implement a comprehensive IPM strategy that combines cultural, mechanical, and chemical control methods to manage varroa mite populations.

2. Screened Bottom Boards: Installing screened bottom boards can help reduce varroa mite populations by allowing mites to fall through the screen and out of the hive.

3. Natural Predators: Encourage the presence of natural varroa mite predators, such as certain species of mite-resistant honeybees or predatory mites, to help control mite populations.

4. Chemical Treatments: Utilize chemical treatments approved for varroa mite control, such as formic acid or oxalic acid, following manufacturer recommendations and safety guidelines.

Small Hive Beetle (Aethina tumida)

Small hive beetles are opportunistic pests that can wreak havoc on weakened or poorly managed honeybee colonies. These beetles lay their eggs in hive debris, where the larvae feed on pollen, honey, and bee brood, causing significant damage and fermentation of hive contents.

Signs of Small Hive Beetle Infestation:

1. Presence of Adult Beetles: Adult small hive beetles may be observed running across comb surfaces or congregating in corners or crevices of the hive.

2. Slimy Residue: Small hive beetle larvae produce a slimy substance as they feed, which can coat hive surfaces and cause honey to ferment.

3. Foul Odor: Infested hives may emit a foul, fermented odor resulting from the decomposition of hive materials by small hive beetle larvae.

4. Damaged Comb: Beetles and their larvae may tunnel through comb, leaving behind gnawed, irregularly shaped galleries.

Management Strategies:

1. Hive Beetle Traps: Deploy beetle traps containing oil or other trapping mechanisms to capture adult beetles and prevent egg-laying within the hive.

2. Maintain Strong Colonies: Ensure that honeybee colonies are healthy and populous, as strong colonies are better equipped to defend against small hive beetle infestations.

3. Good Hive Hygiene: Practice regular hive maintenance, including the removal of excess hive debris and the prompt extraction of surplus honey to minimize opportunities for small hive beetle reproduction.

4. Chemical Controls: Consider using chemical treatments, such as diatomaceous earth or boric acid, in conjunction with other management practices to suppress small hive beetle populations when necessary.

Wax Moths (Galleria mellonella and Achroia grisella)

Wax moths are secondary pests that primarily target weakened or neglected honeybee colonies, exploiting gaps in hive maintenance and sanitation. These moth species lay their eggs in hive comb, where the larvae feed on beeswax, pollen, and other hive materials, causing structural damage and contamination.

Signs of Wax Moth Infestation:

1. Silken Webbing: Wax moth larvae produce silken webbing as they feed, which can be observed covering affected comb surfaces and connecting adjacent cells.

2. Tunnelling Damage: Larvae tunnel through beeswax comb, leaving behind extensive galleries and fecal pellets, which resemble grains of rice.

3. Presence of Adult Moths: Adult wax moths may be seen fluttering around the hive entrance or resting on hive surfaces, particularly during periods of hive weakness or decline.

4. Weak or Abandoned Colonies: Severe wax moth infestations can lead to the weakening or abandonment of honeybee colonies, as bees may abscond in response to the infestation.

Management Strategies:

1. Maintain Strong Colonies: Vigorous, populous colonies are less susceptible to wax moth infestations, as they can effectively defend against moth incursions and repair comb damage.

2. Hive Inspection and Maintenance: Regularly inspect hives for signs of wax moth activity, and promptly remove any infested or damaged comb to prevent the spread of infestation.

3. Freezing: Infested comb can be salvaged by freezing it at temperatures below -18°C (-0.4°F) for at least 48 hours to kill wax moth eggs, larvae, and pupae.

4. Biological Controls: Introduce natural predators of wax moths, such as certain species of parasitic wasps or predatory beetles, to help suppress moth populations in and around the hive.

Conclusion

Monitoring bee health is a fundamental responsibility of every beekeeper. By staying vigilant and proactive in identifying and addressing common pests, you can help ensure the vitality and productivity of your honeybee colonies. Regular hive inspections, coupled with integrated pest management strategies, form the cornerstone of effective pest control in beekeeping. Remember, a healthy hive is a thriving hive, and your efforts in monitoring bee health will be rewarded with robust, resilient colonies capable of weathering the challenges of the beekeeping journey.

2.2 Disease Management

Maintaining the health of your bee colony is paramount for successful beekeeping. Diseases can quickly spread throughout a hive if left unchecked, leading to weakened colonies, decreased honey production, and, in severe cases, hive collapse. Understanding common bee diseases and implementing effective management strategies is essential for ensuring the longevity and productivity of your colony.

Common Bee Diseases

Before delving into disease management techniques, it's crucial to familiarize yourself with the common ailments that can afflict honeybee colonies. Here are some of the most prevalent bee diseases:

American Foulbrood (AFB): AFB is caused by the spore-forming bacterium Paenibacillus larvae. It primarily affects the brood (larvae and pupae) of honeybees and is highly contagious. Infected larvae typically die after their cell is capped, and they turn into dark, gooey masses that emit a foul odor. AFB can decimate entire colonies if not promptly addressed.

European Foulbrood (EFB): Similar to AFB, EFB is a bacterial disease that targets honeybee brood. It is caused by the bacterium Melissococcus plutonius and is characterized by discolored and twisted larvae. Unlike AFB, the brood remains in a semi-solid state and does not produce the same foul odor. However, EFB can still weaken colonies and impair brood development.

Nosema Disease: Nosema is a common fungal infection caused by the microsporidian parasites Nosema apis and Nosema ceranae. These parasites primarily affect adult honeybees' digestive tracts, leading to dysentery, reduced lifespan, and weakened immune systems. Nosema can spread rapidly within a colony, especially during periods of confinement or stress.

Varroosis: Varroosis is caused by the parasitic mite Varroa destructor, which feeds on the bodily fluids of adult bees and developing brood. These mites weaken bees, transmit viruses, and can ultimately lead to colony collapse if left untreated. Varroosis is one of the most significant threats to beekeeping worldwide and requires diligent management practices.

Chalkbrood: Chalkbrood is a fungal disease that primarily affects honeybee larvae. It is caused by the fungus Ascosphaera apis and results in infected larvae becoming mummified and chalk-like in appearance. While chalkbrood typically does not pose a severe threat to colonies, heavy infestations can weaken brood production and hinder colony growth.

Disease Management Strategies

Now that you're familiar with common bee diseases, let's explore effective strategies for managing and preventing their spread within your hive:

Regular Hive Inspections: Conducting routine hive inspections is crucial for early disease detection. During inspections, carefully examine the brood frames for signs of disease, such as abnormal brood patterns, discolored larvae, or foul odors. Promptly address any issues identified during inspections to prevent disease escalation.

Hygienic Beekeeping Practices: Implement hygienic beekeeping practices to minimize disease transmission within your colony. This includes maintaining clean hive equipment, providing adequate ventilation, and practicing good apiary hygiene. Regularly clean and sterilize hive components, such as frames and hive tools, to prevent the buildup and spread of pathogens.

Integrated Pest Management (IPM): Adopt an integrated pest management approach to control common hive pests, such as Varroa mites. IPM combines various strategies, including mechanical, biological, and chemical methods, to manage pest populations while minimizing negative impacts on bees and the environment. Utilize monitoring techniques, such as sticky boards or alcohol washes, to assess Varroa mite infestations and implement targeted treatment measures as needed.

Genetic Selection: Selecting and breeding honeybee colonies with desirable traits, such as hygienic behavior and disease resistance, can help mitigate disease risks. Consider acquiring queen bees from reputable breeders known for breeding disease-resistant stock. Additionally, encourage natural selection by allowing colonies that demonstrate strong disease resistance to propagate through swarm management techniques.

Chemical Treatments: In cases where disease outbreaks cannot be effectively controlled through non-chemical means, judicious use of approved chemical treatments may be necessary. When using chemical treatments, always follow label instructions carefully and adhere to recommended application rates to avoid harming bees or contaminating hive products. Be mindful of potential resistance issues and rotate treatment options to prevent the development of resistant strains.

Collaboration and Education: Stay informed about the latest research and developments in bee health management by participating in beekeeping associations, workshops, and educational events. Collaborate with fellow beekeepers to share knowledge, experiences, and best practices for disease management. By fostering a supportive community, beekeepers can collectively work towards maintaining healthy and resilient bee populations.

Conclusion

Effective disease management is essential for promoting the health and vitality of your bee colony. By implementing proactive monitoring techniques, practicing good hygiene, utilizing integrated pest management strategies, and staying informed about the latest research, you can minimize the impact of common bee diseases and ensure the long-term success of your beekeeping endeavors. Remember, healthy bees are the cornerstone of a thriving apiary and a sustainable future for beekeeping.

3. Seasonal Hive Management

3.1 Spring and Summer

Spring and summer are vital seasons for beekeepers and their hives. During this time, the colony experiences a surge in population and activity as they gather nectar and pollen to build up their resources. Effective hive management during these seasons is crucial for maximizing honey production, preventing swarming, and ensuring the health and vitality of the hive.

3.1.1 Spring Hive Management

Spring marks the beginning of increased bee activity as the temperature rises and flowers begin to bloom. It's a period of rapid growth for the colony, with the queen laying eggs at a prolific rate to expand the population.

Hive Inspections:

Regular hive inspections are essential during spring to assess the colony's condition and address any issues promptly. Inspections should focus on:

- Brood Production: Check for the presence of eggs, larvae, and capped brood. A healthy queen should be laying eggs consistently, and the brood pattern should be even and well-developed.

- Population Size: Evaluate the population size to ensure it's increasing as expected. A thriving colony will have a large workforce to forage and care for brood.

- Queen Health: Verify the presence and health of the queen. Look for signs of queen cells, which may indicate swarming preparations or queen replacement.

- Food Stores: Assess honey and pollen stores within the hive. Ensure there's an ample supply of food to sustain the growing population until the nectar flow increases.

Swarm Prevention:

As the colony expands, the risk of swarming also increases. Swarming is a natural reproductive behavior of honey bee colonies, but it can result in the loss of a significant portion of the workforce and reduce honey production. To prevent swarming:

- Provide Adequate Space: Ensure the hive has sufficient room for brood rearing and honey storage. Add supers as needed to prevent overcrowding.

- Manage Queen Cells: Remove queen cells during inspections to deter the colony from swarming. Alternatively, perform a split to create a new colony and prevent the original hive from swarming.

- Ventilation: Maintain proper ventilation within the hive to prevent overheating, which can trigger swarming behavior.

3.1.2 Summer Hive Management

Summer is characterized by abundant forage opportunities as flowers continue to bloom, providing ample nectar and pollen sources for the bees. However, summer also brings challenges such as heat stress and potential dearth periods in some regions.

Hive Inspections:

During summer, hive inspections should focus on maintaining hive health and productivity amidst the heat and potential dearth conditions. Key areas to address include:

- Supers Management: Continue to monitor honey supers and add additional boxes as necessary to accommodate the honey flow. Regularly extract honey to prevent overcrowding and encourage continued foraging.

- Water Source: Ensure bees have access to a clean water source near the hive to prevent dehydration. Consider providing a water source such as a shallow dish with rocks for bees to land on safely.

- Pest Control: Vigilantly monitor for pests such as Varroa mites and hive beetles, which can proliferate rapidly during summer. Implement appropriate control measures to mitigate infestations and protect hive health.

Hive Ventilation and Cooling:

Summer heat can pose challenges for bee colonies, leading to overheating and decreased productivity. To help bees cope with high temperatures:

- Provide Shade: Place hives in shaded areas or provide artificial shade using umbrellas or shade cloth to reduce direct sunlight exposure.

- Ventilation: Ensure adequate ventilation within the hive by using screened bottom boards and providing upper entrances. This allows hot air to escape and promotes airflow, helping to regulate hive temperature.

Dearth Management:

In some regions, summer may bring periods of reduced nectar flow known as dearths. During dearth periods, bees may struggle to find sufficient forage, leading to decreased honey production and potential stress on the colony. To manage dearths:

- Supplemental Feeding: Consider feeding bees with sugar syrup or fondant during dearth periods to supplement their food stores and prevent starvation.

- Reduce Stress: Minimize disturbances to the hive during dearths to reduce stress on the colony. Avoid unnecessary inspections or manipulations that may disrupt foraging behavior.

3.2 Fall and Winter

As the temperatures drop and nature prepares for the colder months, beekeepers must adjust their hive management practices to ensure the survival and well-being of their colonies during fall and winter. This period presents unique challenges and opportunities for beekeepers, requiring careful attention to hive preparation, pest management, and colony nutrition. In this section, we will delve into the specific tasks and considerations involved in managing hives during the fall and winter seasons.

3.2.1 Fall Hive Preparation

As autumn approaches, beekeepers should begin preparations to help their colonies transition smoothly into the colder months. Fall hive management primarily focuses on ensuring that the bees have sufficient food stores to sustain them through winter, protecting the hive from potential pests and predators, and providing insulation to maintain warmth within the colony.

Assessing Food Stores:

One of the critical tasks in fall hive management is assessing the hive's food stores and supplementing them if necessary. Bees require an adequate supply of honey to sustain them during the winter when foraging opportunities are limited. Conduct a thorough inspection of the hive frames to evaluate the honey reserves. If the hive lacks sufficient honey stores, consider feeding the bees with a sugar syrup solution or providing supplemental feeding with fondant or candy boards. It's essential to monitor the colony's food consumption and adjust feeding as needed to ensure they have enough resources to survive the winter.

Pest Management:

Fall is also a crucial time to address pest management issues to prevent infestations during winter. Varroa mites, in particular, can pose a significant threat to honeybee colonies, especially when bee populations are dwindling in the colder months. Conduct mite assessments using methods such as alcohol washes or powdered sugar rolls and implement appropriate treatment measures if mite levels exceed thresholds. Additionally, consider using integrated pest management (IPM) techniques, such as screened bottom boards or essential oil treatments, to control other common pests like wax moths and hive beetles.

Insulating the Hive:

As temperatures drop, it's essential to provide adequate insulation to help the bees maintain warmth within the hive. Insulating materials such as foam boards or quilt boxes can help reduce heat loss and condensation buildup while allowing for proper ventilation. Ensure that the hive entrance remains unobstructed to facilitate airflow while minimizing drafts that could chill the colony. Wrapping the hive with insulation or a moisture barrier can also provide additional protection against the elements, particularly in regions with harsh winters.

3.2.2 Winter Hive Management

Once winter arrives, beekeepers must continue to monitor their hives and provide ongoing support to help the colonies survive until spring. While bee activity decreases significantly during winter, certain management practices are still necessary to address potential challenges and ensure the colony's well-being.

Monitoring Hive Conditions:

Throughout the winter months, periodically check on the hive's condition, weather permitting, to assess the bees' health and food stores. While it's essential to minimize disturbances to the colony during this time, conducting brief inspections can help identify any issues such as dwindling food supplies, moisture buildup, or signs of disease. Use an infrared camera or a stethoscope to listen for activity within the hive without disturbing the bees unnecessarily.

Supplemental Feeding:

In regions where winters are long and resources are scarce, beekeepers may need to provide supplemental feeding to ensure that the colonies have enough food to survive until spring. Consider using candy boards, fondant, or sugar syrup as emergency food sources if the honey stores are depleted or if prolonged cold weather prevents foraging opportunities. Place the supplemental feed close to the cluster where the bees can access it easily without straying too far from the warmth of the cluster.

Managing Moisture:

Moisture control is critical during winter to prevent condensation buildup, which can lead to mold growth, chilling of the colony, and increased susceptibility to diseases such as nosema. Ensure that the hive has adequate ventilation to allow moisture to escape while preventing drafts that could chill the bees. Installing moisture-absorbing materials such as desiccant packs or wood shavings on top of the inner cover can help absorb excess moisture and maintain a drier environment within the hive.

Protecting Against Predators:

Winter also presents challenges from potential predators seeking shelter and food sources, including mice, birds, and other wildlife. Install mouse guards or entrance reducers to prevent rodents from entering the hive, and consider placing metal or plastic baffles around the hive stand legs to deter climbing predators. Regularly inspect the hive surroundings for signs of animal activity and take appropriate measures to deter or remove potential threats to the colony.

Conclusion

Effective hive management during fall and winter is essential for ensuring the survival and vitality of honeybee colonies through the colder months. By carefully preparing hives, monitoring colony health, and addressing potential challenges such as food shortages, pests, and moisture control, beekeepers can help their bees thrive despite the challenges of winter. With proactive management and attention to detail, beekeepers can support their colonies through the seasonal fluctuations and emerge stronger and healthier as spring approaches.

CHAPTER V
Honey Production

1. Harvesting Honey

1.1 When to Harvest

Harvesting honey is one of the most eagerly anticipated tasks for beekeepers. However, timing is crucial to ensure you obtain the best quality honey while also considering the needs of the colony. The decision on when to harvest honey depends on various factors, including the nectar flow, weather conditions, and the readiness of the bees.

Understanding the Nectar Flow

The nectar flow refers to the period when flowers produce nectar abundantly. This typically coincides with the warmer months of the year when flowers are in bloom. Monitoring the nectar flow in your region is essential for determining the optimal time to harvest honey. Beekeepers often keep track of local flowering patterns and consult with other beekeepers or agricultural experts to gauge the intensity and duration of the nectar flow.

Assessing Hive Readiness

Before harvesting honey, it's crucial to assess the readiness of the hive. A strong, healthy colony will be better equipped to replenish its honey stores after harvesting. Here are some signs that indicate a hive is ready for harvest:

- Capped Honey: When bees have finished processing nectar into honey, they cap the cells with beeswax. Capped honey indicates that the moisture content is sufficiently low for storage. Beeswax capping should be uniformly sealed and have a dry appearance.

- Minimal Bee Activity: During a nectar dearth, when there is a shortage of floral resources, bees become more protective of their honey reserves. If you observe minimal bee activity around the hive entrance and little foraging activity, it may be a sign that the bees have surplus honey to spare.

- Weight of Honey Supers: Lift the honey supers gently to assess their weight. A full honey super will feel heavy, indicating a substantial honey yield. However, be cautious not to disturb the hive excessively during this process to avoid disrupting the bees' activities.

Local Climate Considerations

Climate plays a significant role in honey production and harvesting. In regions with distinct seasons, beekeepers often schedule honey harvesting during periods of stable weather conditions. Ideally, harvesting should occur on warm, sunny days when bees are less likely to be agitated and more focused on foraging.

Avoiding Premature Harvest

Harvesting honey prematurely can have negative consequences for both beekeepers and bees. If honey is harvested before it is adequately ripened, it may contain excess moisture, leading to fermentation and spoilage. Additionally, removing honey prematurely can deprive the colony of essential food stores, especially during periods of scarcity.

Conclusion

Determining the optimal time to harvest honey requires careful observation, knowledge of local conditions, and consideration for the well-being of the bee colony. By monitoring the nectar flow, assessing hive readiness, and accounting for climatic factors, beekeepers can ensure a successful and sustainable honey harvest while promoting the health and productivity of their bee colonies.

In the following sections, we will explore various techniques for harvesting honey and processing it to preserve its quality and flavor.

1.2 Techniques for Harvesting

Harvesting honey is one of the most rewarding aspects of beekeeping. Not only does it provide you with delicious, all-natural sweetener, but it also allows you to witness the fruits of your labor firsthand. However, harvesting honey requires careful planning and execution to ensure both the safety of the beekeeper and the well-being of the colony. In this section, we will explore various techniques for harvesting honey, from traditional methods to modern innovations.

Traditional Hand Tools

Before the advent of modern beekeeping equipment, beekeepers relied on simple hand tools to harvest honey. One of the oldest and most widely used tools is the bee smoker. By puffing smoke into the hive, beekeepers can calm the bees and make them less likely to sting during the harvesting process. Another essential tool is the hive tool, a multipurpose instrument used to pry apart hive components and scrape away excess propolis.

To harvest honey using traditional hand tools, begin by smoking the hive entrance and wait a few minutes for the bees to calm down. Next, carefully remove the hive cover and any inner covers or queen excluders, being mindful not to crush any bees in the process. Then, gently lift out the frames containing capped honeycomb and brush off any bees clinging to the surface. Finally, transport the frames to a designated harvesting area for further processing.

1. Prepare your beekeeping equipment: Put on your protective beekeeping suit, veil, gloves, and smoker. Ensure that your hive tool and other necessary tools are readily accessible.

2. Approach the hive: Approach the hive calmly and quietly, avoiding sudden movements that may agitate the bees.

3. Smoke the hive: Light your smoker and puff smoke gently at the entrance of the hive to calm the bees.

4. Remove the hive cover: Carefully lift the hive cover, inner covers, and any queen excluders, setting them aside in a safe place.

5. Inspect the frames: Inspect each frame to determine which ones contain capped honeycomb ready for harvest. Avoid harvesting honey from frames with uncapped or partially capped cells, as the honey may not be fully matured.

6. Remove the frames: Using your hive tool, gently pry apart the frames, being mindful not to crush any bees in the process.

7. Brush off the bees: Use a soft bee brush or fume board to gently brush off any bees clinging to the frames.

8. Transport the frames: Carefully lift out the frames containing capped honeycomb and transfer them to a designated harvesting area.

Crush and Strain Method

The crush and strain method is a simple yet effective technique for harvesting honey, particularly suitable for small-scale beekeepers or hobbyists. This method involves removing the honeycomb from the frames, crushing it to release the honey, and then straining out any impurities before bottling.

To harvest honey using the crush and strain method, start by carefully removing the frames from the hive as described earlier. Once you have the frames, use a sharp knife or uncapping tool to slice off the wax cappings covering the honeycomb cells. Place the uncapped honeycomb in a clean container or bucket and crush it using a honey extractor, potato masher, or any other suitable tool. Once the honeycomb is fully crushed, pour the mixture through a fine mesh strainer or cheesecloth to separate the honey from the wax and other debris. Allow the strained honey to drip into another container for several hours or overnight, then transfer it to storage jars or bottles.

1. Uncap the honeycomb: Place the frames on a stable surface and use a sharp knife or uncapping tool to remove the wax cappings covering the honeycomb cells.

2. Crush the honeycomb: Place the uncapped honeycomb in a clean container or bucket and crush it using a honey extractor, potato masher, or similar tool until the cells are fully broken.

3. Strain the honey: Set up a fine mesh strainer or cheesecloth over another clean container or bucket. Pour the crushed honeycomb mixture through the strainer to separate the honey from the wax and other debris.

4. Allow the honey to drain: Let the strained honey drip through the strainer for several hours or overnight, ensuring that all the honey has been collected.

5. Transfer the honey: Carefully transfer the strained honey to storage jars or bottles using a funnel if necessary.

Honey Extractors

For larger-scale beekeepers or those seeking a more efficient harvesting method, honey extractors offer a convenient solution. Honey extractors are mechanical devices that use centrifugal force to remove honey from the comb without destroying it, allowing beekeepers to reuse the comb for future honey production.

To harvest honey using a honey extractor, begin by uncapping the honeycomb as described earlier. Once the frames are uncapped, load them into the extractor basket, ensuring that they are evenly distributed to maintain balance. Close the lid of the extractor securely and start the machine, gradually increasing the speed to achieve maximum extraction efficiency. As the extractor spins, the honey is forced out of the comb and collects at the bottom of the extractor drum. Once the extraction process is complete, open the drain valve at the base of the drum to release the honey into a collection container.

1. Uncap the honeycomb: Follow the same steps as described above to uncap the honeycomb using a knife or uncapping tool.

2. Load the frames into the extractor: Place the uncapped frames inside the extractor basket, ensuring that they are evenly distributed to maintain balance.

3. Close the extractor: Securely close the lid of the extractor and ensure that it is properly sealed to prevent honey from leaking out during extraction.

4. Start the extraction process: Begin spinning the extractor at a low speed, gradually increasing the speed to achieve maximum extraction efficiency.

5. Drain the honey: Once the extraction process is complete, open the drain valve at the base of the extractor drum to release the honey into a collection container.

6. Filter the honey: If desired, pour the extracted honey through a fine mesh strainer or cheesecloth to remove any remaining impurities.

7. Transfer the honey: Carefully transfer the filtered honey to storage jars or bottles using a funnel if necessary.

Flow Hive System

In recent years, the introduction of innovative beekeeping technologies such as the Flow Hive system has revolutionized the way honey is harvested. Developed by father-son duo Stuart and Cedar Anderson, the Flow Hive features specially designed frames with pre-formed channels that allow honey to flow directly from the hive into a collection jar with minimal disturbance to the bees.

To harvest honey using the Flow Hive system, simply insert a specially designed key into the frame and turn it to open the channels. As the channels open, the honey flows out of the comb and into a sealed collection jar located beneath the hive. Once the jar is filled with honey, replace it with an empty jar and close the channels to allow the bees to refill the comb.

While the Flow Hive system offers unparalleled convenience and minimal disruption to the bees, it is essential to monitor hive health regularly and ensure that the bees have enough resources to sustain themselves, especially during periods of high honey production.

1. Prepare the Flow Hive: Ensure that the Flow Frames are properly installed and aligned within the hive body, with the collection jars securely in place beneath the frames.

2. Insert the Flow Key: Insert the Flow Key into the designated slots on each frame and turn it to open the channels for honey flow.

3. Monitor the honey flow: Keep an eye on the collection jars to gauge the rate of honey flow. Depending on environmental factors and hive conditions, honey may flow steadily or intermittently.

4. Replace the collection jars: Once a collection jar is filled with honey, replace it with an empty jar and close the channels using the Flow Key to allow the bees to refill the comb.

5. Harvest the honey: When the honey flow has ceased, remove the Flow Frames from the hive and inspect them to ensure that all channels are closed. Carefully remove the filled collection jars and replace them with fresh jars for future harvests.

Conclusion

Regardless of the harvesting method you choose, it is essential to approach the process with care and respect for the bees and their environment. By following proper techniques and guidelines, you can enjoy a bountiful harvest of honey while maintaining the health and well-being of your bee colony. Experiment with different methods and find the approach that works best for you and your bees, keeping in mind the ultimate goal of sustainable and bee-friendly beekeeping practices.

Now that you have learned about the various techniques for harvesting honey, the next step is to explore the process of processing honey, from extracting and filtering to bottling and storing. Join us in the next section as we delve into the fascinating world of honey processing and discover the many uses for this golden liquid and its byproduct, beeswax.

2. Processing Honey

2.1 Extracting Honey

Extracting honey is a crucial step in the honey production process, ensuring that the honey is separated from the comb and ready for consumption or further processing. This task requires careful attention to detail and the use of specialized equipment. In this section, we will explore the various methods and equipment used for extracting honey efficiently while maintaining its quality and purity.

Equipment for Extracting Honey:

1. Extractor: The extractor is the primary piece of equipment used for extracting honey from the comb. It works by centrifugal force, spinning the frames to release the honey from the cells. Extractors come in various sizes, from small manual models suitable for hobbyists to large motorized versions for commercial operations.

2. Uncapping Knife: Before placing the frames in the extractor, the wax cappings covering the honeycomb cells must be removed. An uncapping knife, either heated or cold, is used for this purpose. Heated knives make the process faster by melting through the wax, while cold knives rely on sharp blades to cut through the cappings.

3. Uncapping Tank: As the wax cappings are removed, they need to be collected for processing into beeswax. An uncapping tank is a container designed to catch the cappings and any excess honey that drips off during the uncapping process.

4. Strainer or Sieve: Once the honey is extracted from the comb, it may contain small particles of wax or other debris. A strainer or sieve is used to filter out these impurities, ensuring that the honey is clean and clear.

5. Settling Tank: After straining, the honey is often allowed to sit in a settling tank for a period of time. This allows any air bubbles or foam to rise to the surface and be skimmed off, resulting in a smoother, more aesthetically pleasing product.

Steps for Extracting Honey:

1. Preparation: Before beginning the extraction process, ensure that all equipment is clean and in good working order. The frames containing capped honey should be removed from the hive and transported to the extraction area with care to avoid damaging the delicate comb.

2. Uncapping: Using an uncapping knife, carefully remove the wax cappings from both sides of the frames, exposing the honey-filled cells underneath. Take care to remove only the top layer of wax, leaving the comb intact for reuse by the bees.

3. Loading the Extractor: Once uncapped, the frames are loaded into the extractor. Depending on the size and design of the extractor, multiple frames may be loaded at once. It's essential to balance the extractor by placing frames of equal weight opposite each other to prevent wobbling during the spinning process.

4. Spinning: With the frames securely in place, start the extractor and gradually increase the speed to spin the frames. The centrifugal force causes the honey to be forced out of the cells and collect at the bottom of the extractor's drum or tank.

5. Draining: As the honey is extracted, it flows down the sides of the extractor and collects at the bottom. Open the honey gate or valve to allow the honey to drain out into a collection container or directly into a filtering system.

6. Filtering: Once drained, the honey may pass through a strainer or sieve to remove any remaining wax particles or other impurities. This step helps ensure that the honey is clean and free from debris.

7. Settling: Transfer the filtered honey to a settling tank and allow it to sit for a period of time, typically 24 to 48 hours. During this time, any air bubbles or foam will rise to the surface and can be skimmed off, leaving behind clear, sediment-free honey.

8. Bottling: After settling, the honey is ready to be bottled or jarred for storage and consumption. Use clean, sterilized containers and fill them carefully to avoid introducing air bubbles into the honey.

Tips for Successful Honey Extraction:

1. Work Efficiently: Honey extraction can be time-consuming, especially for large quantities. Work systematically and efficiently to minimize the time between uncapping the frames and bottling the honey to preserve its freshness and quality.

2. Maintain Hygiene: Keep all equipment clean and sanitized to prevent contamination of the honey. Wash hands thoroughly before handling honey or equipment, and use food-grade cleaning products where necessary.

3. Handle with Care: Honey is a delicate product that can be easily damaged or contaminated if mishandled. Avoid vigorous shaking or agitation during extraction and bottling to prevent crystallization or air bubbles from forming.

4. Store Properly: Once bottled, store honey in a cool, dry place away from direct sunlight. Proper storage helps preserve the flavor and consistency of the honey and prevents crystallization over time.

By following these steps and guidelines, beekeepers can extract honey from their hives efficiently while maintaining the quality and purity of the final product. Whether for personal consumption or commercial sale, properly extracted and processed honey is a delicious and nutritious treat enjoyed by people around the world.

2.2 Filtering and Bottling

Filtering honey is a critical step in the processing phase, as it removes foreign particles, such as beeswax, bee parts, and other debris, while also improving the clarity and texture of the final product. Bottling, on the other hand, involves transferring the filtered honey into containers suitable for storage, sale, or personal use. Let's explore these two aspects in detail:

Filtering Honey:

Filtering honey is a relatively straightforward yet essential process that ensures the removal of unwanted substances without compromising the honey's natural properties. Here's a step-by-step guide on how to filter honey effectively:

1. Allow the Honey to Settle: Before filtering, allow the harvested honey to settle for a period, typically 24 to 48 hours. During this time, any air bubbles or foam will rise to the surface, making it easier to skim them off before filtering.

2. Choose the Right Equipment: Select appropriate filtering equipment based on your production scale and preferences. Common filtering tools include stainless steel or nylon mesh strainers, cheesecloths, or fine-mesh sieves.

3. Set Up Your Filtering Station: Prepare a clean and sanitized workspace for filtering. Ensure that all equipment, including containers, filters, and utensils, are thoroughly cleaned to prevent contamination.

4. Filter the Honey: Place your chosen filter over a clean container or bucket and pour the settled honey through it. Depending on the level of filtration desired, you may need to use multiple layers of filters or different mesh sizes to achieve the desired clarity.

5. Monitor the Filtering Process: As the honey passes through the filter, periodically check for clogs or blockages and adjust the filtering setup accordingly. It's essential to maintain a steady flow of honey while ensuring thorough filtration.

6. Collect the Filtered Honey: Once the honey has passed through the filter, collect it in clean, food-grade containers suitable for bottling. Avoid using containers made of reactive materials that may affect the honey's quality.

7. Optional: Heat Treatment (Pasteurization): Some beekeepers choose to heat-treat honey to reduce crystallization and eliminate any potential yeast or bacteria. However, this process may also alter the honey's flavor and nutritional properties, so it's essential to weigh the pros and cons before proceeding.

By following these steps, you can effectively filter your honey, resulting in a clean, clear, and market-ready product. Now, let's turn our attention to the next crucial step: bottling.

Bottling Honey:

Bottling honey is the final step in the processing journey, where the filtered honey is transferred into containers for storage, distribution, or sale. Proper bottling not only preserves the honey's freshness but also enhances its visual appeal and marketability. Here's how to bottle honey like a pro:

1. Select Suitable Containers: Choose containers that are clean, food-grade, and appropriate for the quantity of honey being bottled. Common options include glass jars, plastic squeeze bottles, or bulk containers for larger quantities.

2. Clean and Sanitize: Before bottling, ensure that the chosen containers are thoroughly cleaned and sanitized to prevent contamination. Remove any residues or labels and sterilize the containers using hot water or a food-safe sanitizer.

3. Fill the Containers: Carefully pour the filtered honey into the selected containers, leaving some headspace at the top to accommodate expansion and prevent leakage. Use a funnel or pouring spout to minimize spills and maintain cleanliness.

4. Labeling and Sealing: Once filled, label each container with essential information, such as the honey variety, harvest date, and any relevant nutritional or production details. Seal the containers securely to preserve freshness and prevent tampering.

5. Storage and Distribution: Store the bottled honey in a cool, dry place away from direct sunlight and extreme temperatures to maintain its quality and prevent crystallization. If intending to sell or distribute the honey, ensure compliance with local regulations regarding labeling, packaging, and food safety standards.

6. Marketing and Presentation: Consider the visual presentation of your honey bottles, as attractive packaging can significantly impact consumer perception and sales. Experiment with labeling, branding, and packaging designs to distinguish your product in the market.

7. Quality Control: Regularly inspect bottled honey for signs of crystallization, fermentation, or spoilage. Conduct taste tests and visual inspections to ensure that the honey maintains its quality and flavor over time.

By following these guidelines, you can bottle honey effectively, creating a premium product that appeals to consumers and reflects the dedication and craftsmanship of your beekeeping efforts.

Conclusion:

Processing honey, including filtering and bottling, is a crucial aspect of beekeeping that ensures the quality, purity, and marketability of the final product. By employing proper techniques and attention to detail, beekeepers can produce honey that not only delights the palate but also meets the highest standards of hygiene and food safety. Whether for personal enjoyment, local sale, or commercial distribution, well-processed honey is a testament to the skill and dedication of beekeepers worldwide.

As you embark on your honey processing journey, remember to prioritize cleanliness, quality, and sustainability at every step. By caring for your bees and honoring the natural bounty they provide, you contribute to the preservation of bee populations and the continued enjoyment of honey for generations to come. Happy processing, and may your honey be as sweet as the labor of love that produced it.

3. Uses for Honey and Beeswax

3.1 Culinary Uses

Honey, often referred to as "liquid gold," has been a staple in culinary practices for millennia. Its unique flavor profiles, natural sweetness, and myriad of health benefits make it a versatile ingredient in various cuisines around the world. From sweetening beverages to enhancing savory dishes, honey's uses in the kitchen are endless. In this section, we'll delve into the diverse culinary applications of honey and explore how you can incorporate this delicious nectar into your cooking repertoire.

Sweeteners and Substitutes

One of the most common culinary uses of honey is as a natural sweetener. Unlike refined sugar, honey offers not only sweetness but also depth of flavor. Its distinct floral notes and nuances depend on the nectar collected by bees, resulting in a wide range of honey varieties with unique taste profiles. Whether you prefer the delicate floral notes of acacia honey or the robust flavor of buckwheat honey, there's a type of honey to suit every palate.

In addition to its flavor, honey's natural composition makes it an ideal substitute for sugar in various recipes. Its high viscosity and hygroscopic properties contribute to moisture retention, making it particularly suitable for baking. When substituting honey for sugar in recipes, keep in mind that honey is sweeter than sugar, so you'll need less of it to achieve the same level of sweetness. As a general rule of thumb, use about ¾ to 1 cup of honey for every cup of sugar and reduce the amount of liquid in the recipe by approximately ¼ cup for every cup of honey used.

Breakfast Delights

Honey's versatility extends to the most important meal of the day – breakfast. From drizzling it over pancakes and waffles to stirring it into yogurt or oatmeal, honey adds a touch of natural sweetness and flavor complexity to breakfast dishes. For a nutritious and satisfying start to your day, try topping your morning toast with a generous spread of honey and a sprinkle of cinnamon or pairing Greek yogurt with fresh fruit and a drizzle of honey for a wholesome breakfast bowl.

In addition to sweet dishes, honey can also complement savory breakfast options. Incorporate honey into homemade granola for a hint of sweetness or use it as a glaze for breakfast meats such as bacon or ham. The subtle sweetness of honey balances the saltiness of the meat, creating a harmonious flavor combination that's sure to tantalize your taste buds.

Salad Dressings and Marinades

Honey's versatility shines in salad dressings and marinades, where it serves as both a natural sweetener and a binding agent. Combine honey with olive oil, vinegar, and Dijon mustard for a classic vinaigrette that pairs beautifully with leafy greens, roasted vegetables, or grilled meats. The sweetness of honey balances the acidity of the vinegar, while its viscosity helps emulsify the dressing for a smooth and luscious texture.

In marinades, honey acts as a tenderizing agent, helping to break down proteins and infuse meat, poultry, or seafood with flavor. Create a simple marinade by combining honey with soy sauce, garlic, ginger, and a splash of citrus juice for a sweet and savory glaze that's perfect for grilling or roasting. Whether you're marinating chicken skewers for a barbecue or glazing salmon fillets for a dinner party, honey adds depth and complexity to your culinary creations.

Desserts and Baked Goods

No discussion of culinary uses for honey would be complete without mentioning its indispensable role in desserts and baked goods. From cakes and cookies to pies and pastries, honey lends its unique flavor and moisture-enhancing properties to a wide range of sweet treats. Substitute honey for sugar in your favorite baking recipes to impart a subtle floral aroma and a moist, tender crumb to your creations.

Honey's natural humectant properties also help extend the shelf life of baked goods, keeping them fresh and moist for longer periods. Add a drizzle of honey to fruit crisps and crumbles for an extra layer of sweetness and caramelization, or use it to sweeten whipped cream and frostings for a luscious finishing touch. Experiment with different honey varieties to discover how their distinct flavors can elevate your desserts to new heights of culinary delight.

Beverages and Cocktails

In addition to its culinary applications, honey can also be used to sweeten a variety of beverages, from hot teas and coffees to refreshing cocktails and mocktails. Stir honey into your morning cup of tea or coffee for a natural sweetener that enhances the flavor of your favorite brew. For a refreshing summer beverage, mix honey with lemon juice and water to create a homemade lemonade that's bursting with flavor.

Honey's viscosity makes it an ideal sweetener for cocktails, where it adds depth and complexity to both classic and contemporary libations. Use honey syrup (a mixture of honey and water) as a substitute for simple syrup in cocktails like the Bee's Knees or the Gold Rush for a unique twist on traditional recipes. Experiment with different honey varieties to discover how their nuanced flavors can enhance the complexity of your cocktails and elevate your mixology game.

In conclusion, honey's culinary uses are as diverse as they are delicious. Whether you're sweetening your morning cup of tea, glazing a roast chicken, or baking a batch of cookies, honey adds a touch of natural sweetness and flavor complexity to a wide range of dishes and beverages. So go ahead, explore the culinary wonders of honey, and let your creativity in the kitchen soar to new heights with this golden elixir from the hive.

3.2 Craft and Cosmetic Uses

When we think of honey and beeswax, we often envision delicious recipes or soothing balms. However, their potential reaches far beyond the kitchen or medicine cabinet. Crafters and cosmetic enthusiasts have long prized these natural ingredients for their versatility and effectiveness. In this section, we will explore the myriad ways in which honey and beeswax can elevate your crafting and beauty routines.

Crafting with Beeswax

Beeswax is a staple in many crafting projects due to its malleability, pleasant aroma, and natural properties. Whether you're a seasoned crafter or a novice looking to explore new avenues, beeswax can add a touch of charm and functionality to your creations.

Candle Making: Perhaps the most well-known use of beeswax in crafting is candle making. Beeswax candles are prized for their clean burn and sweet fragrance. To make your own beeswax candles, you'll need beeswax sheets or pellets, wicks, and optionally, essential oils for scent. Simply melt the beeswax, add any desired fragrance, pour it into molds with wicks, and allow it to cool. The result? Beautiful, natural candles that imbue your space with warmth and ambiance.

DIY Beauty Products: Beyond its medicinal properties, beeswax is a popular ingredient in homemade beauty products. Its emollient and protective qualities make it an excellent base for lip balms, lotions, and creams. By combining beeswax with nourishing oils like coconut or almond oil and soothing ingredients like shea butter or cocoa butter, you can create luxurious skincare products tailored to your skin's needs. Experiment with different ratios and additives to find the perfect formula for your DIY creations.

Artisanal Soap Making: Soap making is another craft where beeswax shines. While it's not typically the main ingredient in soap, beeswax can be added to soap recipes to increase hardness and longevity. Additionally, beeswax adds a subtle honey scent and produces a creamy lather, enhancing the overall bathing experience. Incorporate beeswax into your soap making process by melting it with oils and lye, then pouring the mixture into molds to set. The result is artisanal soap bars that nourish the skin while delighting the senses.

Encaustic Painting: For the more artistically inclined, encaustic painting offers a unique way to incorporate beeswax into your creative endeavors. Encaustic painting involves melting beeswax with resin and pigment to create a colorful, textured medium for artistic expression. Artists can manipulate the molten wax with brushes or other tools, building layers and adding depth to their compositions. The wax dries quickly, capturing brushstrokes and creating a luminous, translucent finish that sets encaustic painting apart from other mediums.

Cosmetic Uses of Honey

Honey has been revered for its skincare benefits for centuries, thanks to its natural antibacterial, humectant, and antioxidant properties. From nourishing masks to gentle cleansers, honey can transform your skincare routine, leaving your skin glowing and rejuvenated.

Moisturizing Face Mask: One of the simplest ways to harness the benefits of honey for your skin is by using it as a moisturizing face mask. Raw honey is rich in enzymes and vitamins that nourish and hydrate the skin, making it an ideal treatment for dry or dehydrated skin.

To create a honey mask, simply apply a thin layer of raw honey to clean, damp skin and leave it on for 15-20 minutes before rinsing with warm water. Your skin will be left feeling soft, smooth, and refreshed.

Acne Treatment: Despite its sticky texture, honey can actually help combat acne and blemishes. Its antibacterial and anti-inflammatory properties make it effective at reducing...

CHAPTER VI
Expanding Your Apiary

1. Splitting Hives

1.1 When and Why to Split

Splitting hives is a fundamental practice in beekeeping, essential for both the health of your existing colonies and the growth of your apiary. In this section, we'll delve into the intricacies of splitting hives, exploring when and why to split, as well as various techniques for successful hive division.

Splitting a hive involves creating two or more separate colonies from a single one. Knowing when and why to split is crucial for beekeepers to ensure the continued vitality of their bee colonies and to prevent issues such as overcrowding, swarming, or the spread of diseases.

Here, we'll discuss the key factors that determine the optimal time for hive splitting and the reasons behind this essential practice.

Optimal Timing for Splitting:

1. Population Growth: One of the primary reasons for splitting a hive is to manage population growth. As the bee population in a hive expands, it can lead to overcrowding, which may trigger swarming behavior. Swarming is the natural process by which a colony reproduces, with a portion of bees, including the old queen, leaving the hive to establish a new one. By splitting the hive before swarming occurs, beekeepers can prevent the loss of bees and maintain control over the process.

2. Springtime: Spring is typically the optimal time for splitting hives. As the weather warms up and floral resources become abundant, bee colonies experience rapid population growth and increased foraging activity. Splitting hives during this period allows the newly formed colonies to build up their strength and resources during the peak nectar flow, setting them up for success in the upcoming season.

3. Swarm Prevention: Splitting hives is an effective method for swarm prevention. When a hive becomes overcrowded, bees may start building queen cells, a sign that they are preparing to swarm. By splitting the hive and providing adequate space for the bees to expand, beekeepers can alleviate congestion and reduce the likelihood of swarming.

4. Colony Health: Splitting hives also plays a role in maintaining colony health. It allows beekeepers to identify and address issues such as disease or pest infestations before they spread to other colonies. By dividing the hive, beekeepers can isolate and treat affected colonies, preventing the transmission of pathogens and ensuring the overall well-being of their apiary.

5. Queen Replacement: Splitting hives provides an opportunity for queen replacement. If a hive has a weak or failing queen, beekeepers can create a new colony with a queen cell or

introduce a mated queen to the split hive, ensuring the continued productivity and strength of the colony.

Reasons for Splitting:

1. Swarm Control: As mentioned earlier, splitting hives helps control swarming, which can otherwise deplete the parent colony and lead to a loss of productivity.

2. Colony Expansion: Splitting allows beekeepers to expand their apiary by creating new colonies from existing ones, increasing the overall honey production and genetic diversity of the apiary.

3. Disease Management: Splitting hives facilitates the management of diseases and pests by isolating affected colonies and preventing the spread of pathogens to healthy ones.

4. Genetic Diversity: Creating new colonies through splitting promotes genetic diversity within the apiary, which is essential for the long-term health and resilience of bee populations.

5. Queen Rearing: Splitting hives is an integral part of queen rearing, enabling beekeepers to raise new queens for colony replacement or expansion.

In conclusion, knowing when and why to split hives is crucial for beekeepers to maintain healthy and productive colonies. By understanding the optimal timing and reasons for splitting, beekeepers can effectively manage their apiary, prevent swarming, and promote the well-being of their bees.

In the following sections, we will explore various techniques for splitting hives, providing beekeepers with practical guidance on how to divide their colonies successfully.

1.2 Techniques for Splitting

Splitting hives is a fundamental aspect of beekeeping, essential for colony management, expansion, and swarm prevention. However, it requires precision, timing, and careful execution to ensure the health and productivity of both parent and offspring colonies. In this section, we will delve into various techniques for splitting hives effectively.

1. Timing is Key

Before delving into specific techniques, it's crucial to understand the importance of timing in hive splitting. Timing is not only about the season but also about the strength of the colonies involved. Ideally, splitting should be done during the spring or early summer when colonies are strong and populations are booming. This timing ensures that both the parent and split colonies have ample time to establish themselves before the onset of winter.

2. Equipment Preparation

Before starting the splitting process, gather all the necessary equipment. This includes additional hive bodies, frames, bottom boards, inner and outer covers, entrance reducers, and feeders if required. Having everything prepared in advance streamlines the process and minimizes disruptions to the bees.

3. Selecting the Parent Colony

When choosing which hive to split, select a strong, healthy colony with an abundance of worker bees, brood, pollen, and honey reserves. It's crucial to ensure that the parent colony is robust enough to sustain itself and the split. Avoid splitting weak or struggling colonies, as they may not recover from the division.

4. Splitting Methods

There are several methods for splitting hives, each with its own advantages and considerations. The choice of method often depends on the beekeeper's preferences, resources, and the specific circumstances of the apiary. Some common techniques include:

a. Simple Division

Simple division, also known as the walk-away split, is one of the easiest methods of hive splitting. To perform a simple division, the beekeeper locates the queen in the parent colony and moves her along with several frames of brood, honey, and pollen to a new hive body. The remaining bees in the parent colony will raise a new queen from eggs or young larvae left behind. This method is straightforward but may result in a temporary reduction in honey production as both colonies rebuild their populations.

1. Locate the queen in the parent colony.

2. Move the queen along with several frames of brood, honey, and pollen to a new hive body.

3. Ensure that the new hive has sufficient frames with foundation or drawn comb.

4. Place the new hive in a suitable location away from the parent colony.

5. Leave the remaining bees in the original hive, which will raise a new queen from eggs or young larvae.

b. Demaree Method

The Demaree method is a more intricate approach to hive splitting that involves redistributing frames within the existing hive rather than physically separating colonies.

In this method, the brood nest is divided into upper and lower sections, with the queen and most of the brood placed in the upper section along with frames of honey and pollen. The lower section is left with primarily nurse bees and empty frames. This technique can help manage swarm behavior and maintain honey production while still increasing colony numbers.

1. Conduct a thorough inspection of the hive to assess the distribution of brood, honey, and pollen.

2. Divide the brood nest into upper and lower sections by placing a queen excluder between two deep hive bodies.

3. Move the queen and most of the brood to the upper section along with frames of honey and pollen.

4. Ensure that the lower section has enough nurse bees to care for the remaining brood.

5. Monitor both sections closely and adjust the placement of frames as needed to maintain balance and prevent swarming.

c. Artificial Swarm

The artificial swarm method simulates the natural swarming process by physically dividing the hive into two separate colonies. To perform an artificial swarm, the beekeeper locates the queen in the parent colony and moves her along with a portion of the worker bees and brood to a new hive location. The remaining bees in the original hive will raise a new queen from existing brood. This method effectively prevents swarming while creating a new colony, but it requires careful management to ensure that both colonies have adequate resources to thrive.

1. Locate the queen in the parent colony.

2. Move the queen along with a portion of the worker bees and brood to a new hive location.

3. Ensure that the new hive has adequate resources, including frames of brood, honey, and pollen.

4. Leave the remaining bees in the original hive, which will raise a new queen from existing brood.

5. Provide supplemental feeding if necessary to support both the parent and split colonies during the transition period.

5. Monitoring and Management

After splitting the hive, diligent monitoring and management are essential to the success of both the parent and split colonies. Check both colonies regularly for signs of queen emergence, brood development, pest and disease issues, and overall hive health. Provide supplemental feeding if necessary, especially for newly established splits with limited food reserves. Additionally, consider reuniting colonies if one or both are struggling to thrive independently.

Conclusion

Splitting hives is a valuable skill for beekeepers, allowing for colony expansion, swarm prevention, and overall hive management. By employing the right techniques and timing, beekeepers can successfully split hives while promoting the health and productivity of their apiaries. Remember to adapt techniques based on individual hive conditions and consult with experienced beekeepers or local beekeeping associations for additional guidance and support. With practice and patience, hive splitting can become a rewarding aspect of the beekeeping journey, contributing to the sustainability and growth of bee populations worldwide.

2. Raising Queens

2.1 Importance of a Strong Queen

The queen bee is the heart and soul of a honeybee colony. She is the matriarch, the leader, and the sole egg-layer responsible for the colony's survival and growth. The importance of a strong queen cannot be overstated in the world of beekeeping. In this section, we'll delve into why having a robust and healthy queen is vital for the overall well-being of your apiary.

1. Genetics and Traits Transmission

A strong queen possesses desirable genetic traits that are crucial for the colony's success. These traits include disease resistance, hygienic behavior, productivity, gentleness, and overwintering ability. When a queen mates with drones from diverse genetic backgrounds, she increases the genetic diversity of the colony, which enhances its resilience to environmental stressors and diseases.

2. Egg-Laying Capacity

One of the primary roles of the queen bee is to lay eggs, ensuring the continuous replenishment of the colony's population. A strong queen exhibits a high egg-laying capacity, which is essential for colony expansion and honey production. With a prolific queen, the colony can quickly build up its worker population, allowing for efficient foraging and resource gathering.

3. Colony Stability and Dynamics

The presence of a strong queen stabilizes the colony dynamics by maintaining a balanced ratio of worker bees, drones, and brood. A queen that lays consistently and uniformly spaced eggs regulates the colony's population, preventing overcrowding or underpopulation issues. This, in turn, promotes harmony within the hive and minimizes the likelihood of swarming—a natural reproductive behavior of honeybee colonies.

4. Brood Health and Development

The health and vitality of the brood largely depend on the queen's reproductive performance. A strong queen lays fertilized eggs that develop into healthy larvae, pupae, and eventually emerge as robust adult bees. The quality of brood directly impacts the colony's strength, disease resistance, and productivity. A queen with a genetic predisposition for hygienic behavior ensures that diseased or unhealthy brood are promptly identified and removed, maintaining the overall health of the colony.

5. Colony Resilience

In the face of environmental challenges, such as pests, pathogens, pesticides, and habitat loss, colony resilience becomes paramount for survival. A strong queen contributes to colony resilience by producing offspring with enhanced genetic traits that confer resistance to prevalent threats. By continuously replenishing the worker population with healthy and resilient bees, the colony can better withstand adverse conditions and bounce back from setbacks.

6. Honey Production and Hive Productivity

Ultimately, the strength of a colony underpins its honey production and overall productivity. A strong queen ensures the efficient utilization of resources by maintaining a robust workforce of foragers, nurses, and builders. With ample numbers of worker bees, the colony can effectively collect nectar, process it into honey, rear brood, and maintain the hive infrastructure. This results in higher honey yields and increased profitability for the beekeeper.

Conclusion

In summary, the importance of a strong queen in beekeeping cannot be overstated. From genetics and traits transmission to colony stability, brood health, and honey production, the queen plays a central role in the success and sustainability of the apiary. Beekeepers must prioritize the selection and maintenance of strong queens to ensure the long-term health, productivity, and resilience of their colonies.

In the next section, we will explore various methods for raising queens, empowering beekeepers to cultivate and maintain a robust queen rearing program within their apiaries.

2.2 Methods for Raising Queens

Raising queens is a critical aspect of beekeeping, as the queen bee is the heart of the hive, responsible for laying eggs and maintaining the colony's population. Ensuring you have a strong, healthy queen is essential for the overall success and productivity of your apiary. There are several methods for raising queens, each with its own benefits and considerations. In this section, we will explore some of the most common techniques used by beekeepers to raise queens effectively.

Natural Queen Rearing

Natural queen rearing is perhaps the most hands-off approach to queen production, allowing the bees to raise queens on their own without much human intervention. In this method, the bees select larvae of the appropriate age and condition to raise into queens. Beekeepers can facilitate this process by providing the colony with the conditions conducive to queen rearing, such as an abundance of food and space, as well as a strong and healthy population.

Swarm Cells

Swarm cells are queen cells that bees construct when they intend to swarm, a natural reproductive process of the colony. When the colony becomes overcrowded or conditions are otherwise unfavorable, the bees will create queen cells in preparation for dividing the colony. Beekeepers can take advantage of swarm cells by carefully selecting frames containing these cells and transferring them to new hives or nucleus colonies to raise new queens.

Emergency Queen Cells

Emergency queen cells are created by the bees in response to the sudden loss or decline of the existing queen. When a colony finds itself queenless, either due to the queen's death or failure, the workers will select young larvae and feed them a special diet known as royal jelly to raise emergency queens. Beekeepers can encourage the development of emergency queen cells by providing the colony with a frame of young larvae and ample resources.

Artificial Queen Rearing

Artificial queen rearing involves more direct intervention from the beekeeper and often requires specialized equipment and techniques. While it may be more labor-intensive than natural queen rearing, artificial methods offer greater control over the quality and timing of queen production.

Grafting

Grafting is a popular and widely used method of artificial queen rearing. In grafting, beekeepers manually select young larvae from donor colonies and transfer them to specially prepared queen cups. These queen cups are then placed in a queenless or queenright colony, where nurse bees will care for the larvae and raise them into queens. Grafting allows beekeepers to select larvae of desired genetics and traits, resulting in high-quality queens.

Cloake Board Method

The Cloake Board Method is a technique developed by Harry Cloake for raising queens without the need for grafting. This method involves creating a temporary separation between the queen and the brood chamber using a specially designed board. By controlling access to the queen, beekeepers can manipulate the colony into raising emergency queen cells. Once the queen cells are established, they can be transferred to mating nucs for further development.

Nicot System

The Nicot System is a queen rearing system that utilizes plastic queen cups and cell bars to raise queens. Beekeepers insert cell bars containing queen cups into a queenless colony or mating nuc, where the bees will build queen cells around the cups. Once the queen cells are sealed, they can be harvested and transferred to mating nucs or queenless colonies for mating and eventual emergence as new queens.

Conclusion

Raising queens is a fundamental skill that every beekeeper should master to ensure the health and productivity of their apiary. Whether utilizing natural or artificial methods, the goal remains the same: to produce strong, healthy queens capable of leading thriving colonies. By understanding the various techniques available and selecting the most suitable approach for their circumstances, beekeepers can effectively raise queens and contribute to the sustainability of bee populations worldwide.

3. Adding New Hives

Expanding your apiary is an exciting endeavor in beekeeping, offering opportunities to increase honey production, support pollination efforts, and contribute to the overall health of the bee population. Adding new hives requires careful consideration and planning to ensure the success and sustainability of your beekeeping operation. In this section, we will explore strategies for increasing your colony count, including methods for obtaining new colonies and best practices for hive placement and management.

3.1 Increasing Your Colony Count

Increasing your colony count involves acquiring new bees and establishing additional hives to expand your apiary. There are several methods beekeepers can use to accomplish this, each with its own advantages and considerations.

3.1.1 Buying Package Bees

One common method for increasing colony count is to purchase package bees. Package bees typically consist of a mated queen and a certain number of worker bees, usually ranging from 10,000 to 15,000 bees. These bees are typically sold in screened boxes and can be installed into a hive upon arrival.

When purchasing package bees, it's essential to source them from reputable suppliers to ensure the quality and health of the bees. Look for suppliers who prioritize the well-being of their bees and practice sustainable beekeeping methods. Additionally, consider the genetic diversity of the bees you are purchasing, as genetic diversity is essential for colony resilience and health.

Before installing package bees into a hive, it's crucial to prepare the hive and provide an environment conducive to their success. Ensure the hive is clean, has sufficient food stores, and is free from pests and diseases. Upon installation, monitor the progress of the new colony closely, providing supplemental feeding if necessary and conducting regular hive inspections to assess their health and development.

3.1.2 Capturing Swarm Colonies

Another method for increasing colony count is by capturing swarm colonies. Swarming is a natural reproductive process of honeybee colonies, wherein a portion of the colony, including the queen, leaves the hive to establish a new colony elsewhere. Beekeepers can take advantage of swarms by capturing them and introducing them into their apiary.

To capture a swarm, beekeepers should be vigilant during the swarming season, typically in the spring and early summer. Swarms are often found clustered on tree branches, fence posts, or other structures near their original hive. Once located, the swarm can be gently collected and transferred into a prepared hive.

Capturing swarms offers several benefits, including the acquisition of free bees and the potential to increase genetic diversity within the apiary. However, capturing swarms requires patience, skill, and a willingness to work with bees in outdoor environments. Additionally, beekeepers should be mindful of the potential for swarms to carry diseases or pests, so proper quarantine and inspection protocols should be followed.

3.1.3 Splitting Existing Hives

Splitting existing hives is a method commonly used by beekeepers to increase colony count while also managing hive population and preventing swarming. This method involves dividing a strong, healthy hive into two or more smaller colonies, each with its own queen.

There are several techniques for splitting hives, including the walk-away split and the artificial swarm. In a walk-away split, the beekeeper simply divides the hive into two separate colonies, ensuring that each colony has an adequate number of worker bees, brood, and food stores. The bees will raise a new queen for the colony without a queen, ensuring the continuation of both colonies.

In an artificial swarm, the beekeeper simulates the natural swarming process by creating conditions that prompt the bees to swarm. This typically involves removing the existing queen and a portion of the worker bees from the original hive and placing them in a new hive body at a different location. The original hive is left with queen cells to raise a new queen and replenish its population.

Splitting hives allows beekeepers to increase colony count while also managing hive health and productivity. By dividing strong colonies, beekeepers can prevent overcrowding and swarming while also promoting colony growth and expansion. However, splitting hives requires careful timing and consideration of factors such as hive strength, weather conditions, and resource availability.

3.1.4 Swarm Traps and Bait Hives

In addition to actively seeking out swarms, beekeepers can also use swarm traps and bait hives to attract and capture swarms. Swarm traps are specially designed containers placed in strategic locations to lure passing swarms, while bait hives are fully functional beehives designed to attract swarms seeking a new home.

When setting up swarm traps and bait hives, beekeepers should consider factors such as location, scent attractants, and hive size. Ideal locations for swarm traps and bait hives include areas with high bee activity, such as orchards, meadows, and forest edges. Scent attractants such as lemongrass oil or old brood comb can be used to mimic the pheromones released by a queen bee, attracting passing swarms to investigate the trap or bait hive.

Once a swarm has been captured in a trap or bait hive, beekeepers can transfer the bees into a permanent hive in their apiary. Swarm traps and bait hives offer a passive method for increasing colony count, allowing beekeepers to leverage the natural behavior of honeybee swarms to expand their apiary.

3.1.5 Nucleus Colonies (Nucs)

Nucleus colonies, commonly referred to as nucs, are small, self-contained colonies consisting of a queen, several frames of brood, worker bees, and food stores. Nucs are typically sold by beekeepers or suppliers and can serve as a convenient way to establish new hives or strengthen existing ones.

When purchasing nucs, beekeepers should ensure they are obtaining healthy, disease-free colonies from reputable sources. Nucs offer several advantages, including a head start in colony development, reduced risk of queen failure, and increased chances of overwintering success.

Upon receiving a nuc, beekeepers should transfer the frames into a permanent hive body and provide the necessary care and management to support colony growth and development. This may include supplemental feeding, regular inspections, and pest and disease monitoring.

Nucleus colonies are an excellent option for beekeepers looking to increase colony count quickly and efficiently. By starting with a strong nucleus colony, beekeepers can accelerate the establishment of new hives and enhance the overall productivity and resilience of their apiary.

Conclusion

Increasing your colony count is a fundamental aspect of expanding your apiary and enhancing your beekeeping operation. Whether through purchasing package bees, capturing swarms, splitting existing hives, using swarm traps and bait hives, or acquiring nucleus colonies, beekeepers have a variety of options for adding new hives to their apiary.

Regardless of the method chosen, it's essential to prioritize the health and well-being of the bees, ensuring they have access to adequate food, shelter, and resources. By employing sustainable beekeeping practices and thoughtful management techniques, beekeepers can successfully increase their colony count while supporting the vitality and resilience of their bee populations.

As you embark on the journey of expanding your apiary, remember to approach each new hive with care, attention, and a commitment to the principles of bee-friendly beekeeping. By working in harmony with the bees and their natural instincts, you can create a thriving apiary that not only produces honey and pollinates crops but also contributes to the conservation and protection of these vital pollinators for generations to come.

3.2 Managing Multiple Hives

Managing multiple hives can be both exciting and challenging for beekeepers. As you expand your apiary, you'll need to develop efficient strategies to care for each hive while maintaining their health and productivity. In this section, we'll explore various aspects of managing multiple hives, including organization, monitoring, and troubleshooting common issues.

Organization and Layout

Before diving into the management techniques, it's crucial to establish an organized layout for your apiary. A well-thought-out arrangement not only facilitates hive management but also ensures optimal foraging patterns for your bees.

1. Spacing: Maintain adequate spacing between hives to prevent overcrowding and reduce the risk of disease transmission. A distance of at least three feet between hives is recommended to minimize drifting.

2. Orientation: Position hives with their entrances facing different directions to prevent confusion among foragers returning to the wrong colony. This also helps in optimizing sunlight exposure and airflow for each hive.

3. Accessibility: Ensure easy access to all hives for routine inspections and maintenance tasks. Clear pathways and consider using raised hive stands to elevate hives, making it easier to work around them.

4. Water Source: Place water sources such as shallow trays or birdbaths near the apiary to provide bees with a convenient and reliable water supply, reducing the likelihood of them seeking water from neighboring properties.

Monitoring and Record-Keeping

Regular monitoring is essential for early detection of issues and timely intervention. Keep detailed records of each hive's health, behavior, and productivity to track their progress over time and identify any deviations from the norm.

1. Inspections: Conduct thorough hive inspections at regular intervals, typically once every one to two weeks during the active season. Check for signs of disease, pest infestations, queen performance, and honey production.

2. Data Logging: Utilize hive monitoring technologies such as hive scales, temperature and humidity sensors, and entrance counters to gather real-time data on hive conditions. This data can help you make informed decisions and detect trends that may not be apparent during routine inspections.

3. Notekeeping: Maintain a hive journal or digital logbook to record observations, interventions, and outcomes for each hive. Note important milestones such as queen introductions, honey harvests, and population fluctuations.

4. Communication: Stay connected with other beekeepers in your area through local beekeeping associations or online forums. Sharing experiences and insights can provide valuable support and guidance, especially when facing challenges specific to your region.

Hive Management Practices

Managing multiple hives involves juggling various tasks to ensure the well-being of each colony. Here are some key practices to incorporate into your management routine:

1. Queen Management: Monitor queen performance regularly and replace underperforming or aging queens as needed. Implement queen rearing techniques to maintain a consistent supply of healthy queens for hive expansion or replacement.

2. Disease Prevention: Practice good sanitation and hygiene measures to prevent the spread of diseases between hives. Sterilize hive tools between inspections, avoid sharing

equipment between sick and healthy hives, and quarantine newly acquired bees before introducing them to your apiary.

3. Swarm Prevention: Implement swarm prevention measures such as timely hive inspections, providing adequate space for colony expansion, and performing hive manipulations such as checkerboarding or adding supers to alleviate congestion.

4. Feeding and Supplementation: Monitor hive resources closely, especially during periods of nectar dearth or inclement weather. Provide supplemental feeding using sugar syrup or pollen substitutes to ensure colonies have sufficient food stores for survival and productivity.

5. Integrated Pest Management (IPM): Adopt IPM strategies to manage common pests such as Varroa mites, wax moths, and hive beetles. Use a combination of cultural, mechanical, and biological control methods to minimize reliance on chemical treatments and reduce the risk of resistance development.

Troubleshooting Common Issues

Despite your best efforts, you may encounter challenges while managing multiple hives. Here are some common issues beekeepers face and strategies for addressing them:

1. Weak Colonies: Assess the reasons for colony weakness, such as queen failure, disease, or inadequate resources. Take prompt action to address underlying issues, such as requeening, disease treatment, or supplemental feeding, to strengthen the colony.

2. Queenlessness: If a hive becomes queenless, introduce a mated queen or a queen cell from a strong colony to restore reproductive function and colony cohesion. Monitor the acceptance of the new queen and provide additional support if necessary.

3. Robbing: Take measures to prevent robbing behavior, such as reducing hive entrances, using entrance reducers, or installing robbing screens. Address any weak or vulnerable colonies promptly to minimize the risk of exploitation by neighboring bees.

4. Hive Decline: Investigate the causes of hive decline, which may include disease outbreaks, pesticide exposure, or environmental stressors. Implement remedial actions such as disease treatment, habitat improvement, or relocation if necessary to mitigate further decline.

Conclusion

Managing multiple hives requires careful planning, diligent monitoring, and proactive intervention. By establishing a structured approach to hive management, staying vigilant for signs of issues, and implementing effective management practices, you can maximize the health and productivity of your apiary. Remember to adapt your strategies based on seasonal fluctuations, hive dynamics, and local environmental conditions to achieve long-term success in beekeeping.

CHAPTER VII
Advanced Beekeeping Techniques

1. Natural Beekeeping

1.1 Organic Practices

Organic beekeeping is a philosophy and practice that prioritizes the health and well-being of honeybees while minimizing negative impacts on the environment. It emphasizes natural, sustainable methods of hive management and pest control, avoiding the use of synthetic chemicals and antibiotics. In this section, we will delve into the principles and practices of organic beekeeping, exploring everything from hive management to pest and disease control.

Understanding Organic Beekeeping

Organic beekeeping is rooted in the belief that healthy bees are better equipped to resist pests, diseases, and environmental stressors. By creating an environment that mimics the bees' natural habitat and supports their innate behaviors, organic beekeepers aim to build resilient colonies capable of thriving without human intervention.

At the heart of organic beekeeping are principles such as:

- Respect for the Bees: Organic beekeepers prioritize the well-being of their bees above all else. This means allowing the bees to express their natural behaviors, such as swarming and propolis collection, without interference.

- Natural Hive Materials: Organic beekeepers use natural materials, such as wood, straw, and beeswax, to construct their hives. These materials are free from harmful chemicals and additives, ensuring a safe and healthy environment for the bees.

- Chemical-Free Management: Organic beekeepers avoid the use of synthetic chemicals, pesticides, and antibiotics in hive management. Instead, they rely on non-toxic methods to control pests and diseases, such as integrated pest management (IPM) and selective breeding for resistance.

- Sustainable Beekeeping Practices: Organic beekeepers practice sustainable beekeeping techniques that minimize their impact on the environment. This includes sourcing local, organic feed for the bees, promoting biodiversity in the surrounding landscape, and reducing carbon emissions associated with hive management.

Hive Management

Organic hive management focuses on creating a habitat that supports the bees' natural instincts and behaviors. This includes providing ample space for foraging, minimizing disturbances to the hive, and ensuring good ventilation and drainage. Here are some key practices:

- Natural Comb Construction: Organic beekeepers allow bees to build their comb naturally, without the use of plastic foundation or wires. This encourages the bees to create cell sizes that are best suited to their needs and promotes overall colony health.

- Minimal Intervention: Organic beekeepers limit their interventions in the hive, only inspecting or manipulating the colony when absolutely necessary. This reduces stress on the bees and allows them to regulate their own population, brood, and honey stores.

- Seasonal Management: Organic beekeepers adjust their management practices according to the seasons, taking into account factors such as weather, forage availability, and natural bee biology. This may involve providing supplementary feeding during times of scarcity, insulating hives in cold weather, or providing shade in hot climates.

Pest and Disease Control

Organic beekeepers employ a variety of non-toxic methods to control pests and diseases in their colonies. These methods focus on promoting hive health and resilience, rather than relying on chemical treatments that may harm the bees or contaminate hive products. Here are some common practices:

- Integrated Pest Management (IPM): IPM is a holistic approach to pest control that combines cultural, mechanical, and biological methods to manage pest populations. Organic beekeepers use techniques such as screened bottom boards, drone brood trapping, and natural predators to keep pest levels in check.

- Hygienic Bee Breeding: Organic beekeepers selectively breed for traits such as grooming behavior and hygienic behavior, which help bees resist pests and diseases. This involves identifying colonies with high levels of resistance and propagating their genetics through controlled breeding programs.

- Natural Remedies: Organic beekeepers use natural remedies such as essential oils, organic acids, and powdered sugar dusting to control pests such as Varroa mites and wax moths. These treatments are less harmful to the bees and can be effective when used as part of a comprehensive pest management strategy.

Conclusion

Organic beekeeping offers a sustainable and environmentally friendly approach to beekeeping that prioritizes the health and well-being of honeybees. By embracing natural hive management practices and non-toxic pest control methods, organic beekeepers can create resilient colonies that are better equipped to thrive in today's challenging environment. Whether you're a seasoned beekeeper or just starting out, incorporating organic principles into your beekeeping practice can help support healthy bees and a thriving ecosystem for generations to come.

1.2 Sustainable Methods

In the realm of beekeeping, sustainability has become an increasingly vital consideration. As global awareness of environmental issues grows, so does the recognition of the importance of sustainable practices within the apicultural community. Sustainable beekeeping encompasses a range of techniques and principles aimed at ensuring the long-term health and vitality of both honeybee colonies and the ecosystems in which they reside. In this section, we delve into various sustainable methods employed by conscientious beekeepers around the world.

Integrated Pest Management (IPM)

One cornerstone of sustainable beekeeping is the practice of Integrated Pest Management (IPM). Traditional methods of pest control often rely heavily on the use of chemical pesticides, which can have detrimental effects on bee health and the environment. In contrast, IPM seeks to minimize reliance on synthetic chemicals by employing a multifaceted approach to pest management.

At the heart of IPM is the principle of prevention. Beekeepers utilizing IPM techniques focus on creating conditions that discourage pest infestations in the first place. This may involve strategies such as maintaining strong, healthy colonies, practicing good hive hygiene, and providing bees with a diverse and nutritious diet.

When pests do occur, IPM encourages the use of non-chemical control methods wherever possible. These may include physical interventions such as the removal of infested comb or the use of mechanical traps. Biological control measures, such as introducing natural predators of pest species, can also play a role in an IPM strategy.

Chemical interventions are considered a last resort in IPM and are used sparingly and judiciously. When pesticides are deemed necessary, beekeepers opt for products that are specifically formulated to minimize harm to bees and other non-target organisms. Additionally, timing and application methods are carefully chosen to minimize exposure to bees and their environment.

By adopting an Integrated Pest Management approach, beekeepers can effectively manage pest pressures while minimizing the negative impacts on bee health and the environment. Furthermore, by reducing reliance on chemical pesticides, IPM contributes to the overall sustainability of beekeeping operations.

Habitat Enhancement

Another key aspect of sustainable beekeeping is the promotion of bee-friendly habitats. Honeybees, like many other pollinators, rely on a diverse array of flowering plants for nectar and pollen. However, habitat loss and fragmentation, as well as the widespread use of pesticides, have led to declines in floral resources for bees in many areas.

Sustainable beekeepers work to counteract these trends by actively enhancing and expanding bee-friendly habitat. This may involve planting pollinator-friendly gardens, establishing wildflower meadows, or participating in habitat restoration projects. By providing bees with a diverse and abundant source of forage, beekeepers can help support healthy and resilient honeybee populations.

In addition to providing food for bees, habitat enhancement efforts can also benefit other pollinators and native wildlife, as well as contributing to broader ecosystem health. By creating and preserving biodiverse habitats, sustainable beekeepers play a crucial role in promoting the interconnected web of life on which bees and humans alike depend.

Genetic Diversity

Maintaining genetic diversity within honeybee populations is another important consideration for sustainable beekeeping. Genetic diversity enhances the resilience of honeybee colonies, making them better able to adapt to changing environmental conditions and resist disease and pests.

Unfortunately, many commercial beekeeping operations rely on a limited number of bee breeds or strains, which can lead to a loss of genetic diversity over time. Sustainable beekeepers seek to counteract this trend by selecting and breeding bees for traits such as disease resistance, productivity, and temperament, while also prioritizing the preservation of genetic diversity.

One way beekeepers can promote genetic diversity is by utilizing locally adapted bee stocks. Bees that have evolved in a particular geographic area are often better suited to the local climate and environmental conditions, making them more resilient and productive in that setting.

Additionally, sustainable beekeepers may employ techniques such as selective breeding, genetic testing, and the exchange of genetic material with other beekeepers to enhance genetic diversity within their colonies. By maintaining healthy, genetically diverse honeybee populations, beekeepers can help ensure the long-term viability of their operations and contribute to the conservation of honeybee biodiversity worldwide.

Resource Conservation

Resource conservation is a fundamental principle of sustainable beekeeping. Beekeeping requires various resources, including water, energy, and materials such as wood and wax. Sustainable beekeepers strive to minimize their use of these resources and reduce waste wherever possible.

One area of resource conservation in beekeeping is hive construction. Traditional Langstroth hives, while widely used, require significant amounts of wood and other materials to manufacture. Sustainable beekeepers may opt for alternative hive designs, such as top-bar hives or Warre hives, which use less material and are often easier and less resource-intensive to maintain.

Water usage is another consideration for sustainable beekeepers, particularly in regions where water scarcity is a concern. Providing bees with a clean and reliable water source is essential for colony health, but excessive water consumption can strain local water supplies. Sustainable beekeepers implement water-saving measures such as rainwater harvesting, drip irrigation systems, and the use of water-efficient equipment to minimize their water footprint.

Energy consumption is also a concern for beekeepers, particularly in the operation of honey extraction and processing equipment. Sustainable beekeepers may invest in energy-efficient appliances, utilize renewable energy sources such as solar power, or implement energy-saving practices such as optimizing workflow efficiency and minimizing unnecessary energy use.

By conserving resources and minimizing waste, sustainable beekeepers can reduce their environmental impact and operate more efficiently and cost-effectively in the long term.

Conclusion

Sustainable beekeeping encompasses a range of techniques and principles aimed at promoting the long-term health and vitality of honeybee colonies and the ecosystems in which they reside. By adopting practices such as Integrated Pest Management, habitat enhancement, genetic diversity conservation, and resource conservation, beekeepers can minimize their environmental impact and contribute to the sustainability of beekeeping operations worldwide. Through these efforts, beekeepers play a crucial role in safeguarding the future of honeybees and the invaluable ecosystem services they provide.

2. Migratory Beekeeping

2.1 Benefits and Challenges

Migratory beekeeping, the practice of transporting bee colonies to different locations throughout the year, is a crucial aspect of modern beekeeping, especially in commercial operations. This method allows beekeepers to maximize honey production and provide vital pollination services to various crops. However, it comes with a unique set of benefits and challenges that beekeepers must navigate to ensure the health and productivity of their colonies.

Benefits of Migratory Beekeeping

1. Increased Honey Production:

   One of the primary benefits of migratory beekeeping is the ability to follow nectar flows throughout the year. By moving colonies to regions with abundant floral resources, beekeepers can ensure that their bees have access to continuous nectar sources, leading to higher honey yields. For instance, beekeepers might move their hives to areas with blooming clover in the spring, wildflowers in the summer, and goldenrod in the fall, optimizing honey production.

2. Enhanced Pollination Services:

   Migratory beekeeping plays a vital role in the agricultural industry by providing essential pollination services for various crops. Crops such as almonds, apples, blueberries, and many others rely heavily on honeybees for pollination. By transporting hives to orchards and fields during the blooming period, beekeepers contribute to higher crop yields and improved fruit quality, benefiting farmers and the food supply chain.

3. Diversified Income Streams:

Migratory beekeepers can diversify their income by engaging in both honey production and pollination services. Renting out hives for pollination can be a lucrative business, especially during peak bloom seasons when the demand for pollinators is high. This diversification helps stabilize income and mitigate risks associated with fluctuations in honey prices or poor nectar flows.

4. Disease and Pest Management:

Moving colonies can help manage certain pests and diseases. For example, relocating hives to areas with less Varroa mite pressure or away from regions with known disease outbreaks can help reduce the impact of these threats. Additionally, the break in the brood cycle during transportation can disrupt the life cycle of pests and pathogens, providing a natural form of pest management.

Challenges of Migratory Beekeeping

1. Logistical Complexities:

Migratory beekeeping involves significant logistical planning and coordination. Transporting hives requires specialized equipment, such as flatbed trucks, forklifts, and proper securing mechanisms to ensure the safe and efficient movement of colonies. Beekeepers must also consider the timing of moves to coincide with nectar flows and blooming periods, which can vary widely by region and crop.

2. Stress on Bees:

The process of relocating hives can be stressful for bee colonies. Frequent moves can disrupt the bees' natural behavior, leading to disorientation and reduced productivity. Stress factors such as temperature fluctuations, vibrations during transport, and changes in forage availability can impact colony health. Beekeepers must carefully manage these stressors to maintain strong and productive colonies.

3. Exposure to Pesticides:

Bees in migratory operations are often exposed to a variety of agricultural environments, some of which may have high pesticide usage. Pesticide exposure can have detrimental effects on bee health, leading to colony losses and reduced honey production. Beekeepers must work closely with farmers to ensure that hives are placed in safe locations and that pesticide applications are managed to minimize harm to the bees.

4. Increased Labor and Costs:

Migratory beekeeping is labor-intensive and requires additional financial investment. The costs of transportation, fuel, labor, and equipment maintenance can add up, making this practice more expensive than stationary beekeeping. Beekeepers must weigh these costs against the potential benefits to determine the economic viability of their operations.

5. Regulatory Compliance:

Transporting bees across state or national borders involves compliance with various regulations and inspection requirements. Beekeepers must obtain the necessary permits and health certifications to move their colonies legally. These regulations are designed to prevent the spread of diseases and pests, but they add an additional layer of complexity to migratory beekeeping.

Strategies for Successful Migratory Beekeeping

To mitigate the challenges and maximize the benefits of migratory beekeeping, beekeepers can adopt several strategies:

1. Careful Planning:

Detailed planning is essential for successful migratory beekeeping. Beekeepers should create a schedule that aligns with nectar flows and pollination demands. They should also plan transportation routes and logistics to minimize travel time and stress on the bees.

2. Communication with Farmers:

Building strong relationships with farmers is crucial for ensuring safe and effective pollination services. Beekeepers should communicate regularly with farmers about hive placement, pesticide usage, and bloom periods to protect the health of their colonies.

3. Regular Health Monitoring:

Frequent health checks and monitoring are vital for maintaining strong colonies. Beekeepers should inspect their hives regularly for signs of disease, pests, and stress. Implementing integrated pest management (IPM) practices can help control pest populations and reduce the need for chemical treatments.

4. Use of Technology:

Modern technology can aid in the management of migratory beekeeping operations. GPS tracking, remote hive monitoring systems, and data analytics can provide valuable insights into colony health, forage availability, and environmental conditions, helping beekeepers make informed decisions.

5. Environmental Considerations:

Beekeepers should consider the environmental impact of their operations. Selecting locations with diverse forage and minimal pesticide exposure can improve colony health. Additionally, practicing sustainable beekeeping methods, such as using organic treatments and minimizing chemical inputs, can contribute to healthier bees and ecosystems.

6. Education and Training:

Continuous education and training are essential for staying up-to-date with best practices and advancements in beekeeping. Beekeepers should participate in workshops, conferences, and online courses to enhance their knowledge and skills in migratory beekeeping.

Case Study: Successful Migratory Beekeeping Operation

To illustrate the potential of migratory beekeeping, let's consider a case study of a successful operation. The Smith Family Apiaries, based in California, have been practicing migratory beekeeping for over two decades. They manage a large fleet of hives, moving them across several states to follow nectar flows and provide pollination services.

Operation Overview:

- Locations: The Smiths move their hives between California, Oregon, and Washington, following the bloom periods of almonds, blueberries, and wildflowers.

- Hive Numbers: They manage approximately 2,000 hives, divided into smaller units for ease of transportation and management.

- Pollination Contracts: The Smiths have long-term contracts with several large almond orchards and blueberry farms, providing reliable income from pollination services.

Best Practices:

- Hive Health: The Smiths prioritize hive health by conducting regular inspections and implementing IPM practices. They use organic treatments for Varroa mites and focus on maintaining strong, healthy colonies.

- Logistics: They have invested in specialized equipment, including trucks with climate-controlled compartments, to reduce stress during transportation. Hives are carefully loaded and secured to prevent damage and ensure safe arrival at each location.

- Communication: The Smiths maintain open lines of communication with their farmer partners, discussing hive placement, pesticide use, and bloom timings to optimize pollination and protect their bees.

- Data-Driven Decisions: Utilizing remote monitoring technology, the Smiths track hive conditions and environmental factors in real-time, allowing them to make data-driven decisions about hive movements and management practices.

Outcomes:

- Increased Honey Yields: By following nectar flows, the Smiths achieve high honey yields, producing a variety of honeys with distinct regional flavors.

- Successful Pollination: Their pollination services contribute to significant increases in crop yields and quality, earning them a reputation as reliable pollinators.

- Sustainable Practices: The Smiths' commitment to organic and sustainable beekeeping practices has resulted in healthier bees and reduced environmental impact.

In conclusion, migratory beekeeping offers numerous benefits, including increased honey production, enhanced pollination services, and diversified income streams. However, it also presents challenges such as logistical complexities, stress on bees, and exposure to pesticides. By adopting careful planning, effective communication, regular health monitoring, and sustainable practices, beekeepers can navigate these challenges and achieve successful migratory operations. The case study of the Smith Family Apiaries demonstrates how these strategies can be implemented to create a thriving and sustainable migratory beekeeping business.

2.2 Best Practices

Migratory beekeeping, a practice involving the transportation of beehives to various locations to exploit seasonal floral resources, is both an art and a science. It requires a thorough understanding of bee behavior, floral biology, and logistical management to ensure the health and productivity of the colonies. In this section, we will delve into the best practices that successful migratory beekeepers follow to optimize their operations, minimize stress on the bees, and maintain high levels of honey production and pollination efficiency.

Preparation and Planning

Effective migratory beekeeping starts with meticulous preparation and planning. Before embarking on the journey, beekeepers must:

1. Research Floral Cycles: Understanding the blooming cycles of different plants in various regions is crucial. Beekeepers should study the seasonal availability of nectar and pollen sources to plan the migration routes accordingly. This ensures that the bees always have access to abundant forage, which is essential for their health and productivity.

2. Health Assessment: Prior to moving the hives, conduct a thorough health assessment of the colonies. Check for signs of disease, pests, and overall colony strength. Healthy colonies are more resilient to the stresses of transportation and are better able to capitalize on new forage opportunities.

3. Equipment Maintenance: Inspect all beekeeping equipment, including hives, frames, and transportation tools, to ensure they are in good working condition. Replace any damaged or worn-out components to prevent issues during transit.

4. Legal Considerations: Be aware of and comply with local, state, and federal regulations regarding the transportation of bees. This includes obtaining necessary permits and adhering to quarantine rules to prevent the spread of pests and diseases.

Transportation Logistics

The actual process of transporting bees involves several critical steps to ensure the safety and well-being of the colonies:

1. Timing the Move: Plan the move during cooler parts of the day, such as early morning or late evening, when bees are less active and more likely to stay inside the hive. This reduces the risk of bee loss and stress during transport.

2. Securing the Hives: Properly secure the hives to prevent shifting and damage during transit. Use straps, nets, or other securing mechanisms to keep the hives stable. Ensure adequate ventilation to prevent overheating, especially in warmer climates.

3. Minimizing Vibration: Use vehicles with good suspension systems and drive carefully to minimize vibrations and jolts, which can disturb and stress the bees. Smooth driving reduces the risk of bees becoming agitated or injured.

4. Hydration and Feeding: Provide a source of hydration for the bees during transit, particularly on long journeys. Some beekeepers place soaked sponges or special feeders inside the hives to keep the bees hydrated. Additionally, if the journey is prolonged, consider providing supplementary feeding to ensure the bees have enough energy.

Site Selection

Choosing the right location for the hives upon arrival is critical for the success of migratory beekeeping:

1. Forage Availability: Select sites with abundant and diverse floral resources. Consider the blooming schedule and ensure that there will be a continuous supply of nectar and pollen. Avoid areas with heavy pesticide use, as these can harm the bees.

2. Water Sources: Ensure there is a nearby source of clean water for the bees. Bees need water for drinking, cooling the hive, and diluting honey for consumption.

3. Environmental Conditions: Evaluate the environmental conditions of the site, including temperature, humidity, and wind patterns. Choose locations that provide natural shelter from extreme weather conditions.

4. Accessibility and Security: Ensure the site is easily accessible for regular hive inspections and maintenance. Additionally, consider the security of the location to protect the hives from theft or vandalism.

Hive Management at New Locations

Once the hives are placed at the new location, ongoing management is crucial to maintain colony health and productivity:

1. Regular Inspections: Conduct regular hive inspections to monitor colony health, check for signs of disease or pests, and assess the bees' foraging activity. Early detection of issues allows for prompt intervention.

2. Supplementary Feeding: If natural forage is insufficient, provide supplementary feeding to support the colonies. This can include sugar syrup, pollen substitutes, or protein supplements, especially during dearth periods.

3. Disease and Pest Management: Implement integrated pest management (IPM) strategies to control pests such as Varroa mites, small hive beetles, and wax moths. Use a combination

of cultural, mechanical, and chemical controls to keep pest populations in check without harming the bees.

4. Swarm Prevention: Monitor the hives for signs of swarming, such as queen cells or overcrowding. Use management techniques like splitting colonies or providing additional space to prevent swarming, which can reduce the productivity of the hives.

Record Keeping and Data Analysis

Effective record keeping is an essential component of successful migratory beekeeping:

1. Track Movements: Keep detailed records of hive movements, including dates, locations, and distances traveled. This information helps in planning future migrations and assessing the impact of different locations on colony health and productivity.

2. Monitor Production: Record honey yields, pollen collection, and other production metrics at each location. Analyzing this data allows beekeepers to identify the most productive sites and optimize future migration plans.

3. Health Records: Maintain records of colony health assessments, disease treatments, and pest management interventions. This helps in tracking the effectiveness of different management strategies and ensuring the long-term health of the colonies.

4. Environmental Observations: Document environmental conditions at each site, including weather patterns, forage availability, and any other relevant factors. This information can provide insights into how different conditions impact bee behavior and productivity.

Community and Environmental Impact

Migratory beekeeping has broader implications for both local communities and the environment:

1. Pollination Services: Migratory beekeepers play a crucial role in providing pollination services for various crops. By strategically placing hives in agricultural areas, beekeepers can enhance crop yields and support local food production.

2. Environmental Stewardship: Practice sustainable beekeeping methods to minimize the environmental impact of migratory operations. This includes reducing chemical use, protecting natural habitats, and promoting biodiversity through responsible site selection and management.

3. Community Engagement: Engage with local communities to educate them about the importance of bees and beekeeping. Foster positive relationships with landowners, farmers, and other stakeholders to ensure continued access to prime foraging sites.

Adapting to Challenges

Migratory beekeeping is not without its challenges. Successful beekeepers must be adaptable and proactive in addressing various issues:

1. Weather Variability: Weather patterns can be unpredictable, affecting forage availability and colony behavior. Beekeepers must be prepared to adapt their plans and provide additional support to the colonies during adverse conditions.

2. Pesticide Exposure: Pesticide use in agricultural areas poses a significant risk to bee health. Beekeepers should communicate with farmers to coordinate hive placements and minimize pesticide exposure. Additionally, advocate for bee-friendly pest management practices.

3. Colony Stress: The stress of transportation and frequent relocations can impact colony health. Implement strategies to minimize stress, such as providing ample forage, maintaining strong colonies, and using gentle handling techniques.

4. Market Fluctuations: The profitability of migratory beekeeping can be influenced by market fluctuations in honey prices and demand for pollination services. Diversify income streams by exploring additional products like beeswax, propolis, and bee pollen.

Conclusion

Migratory beekeeping is a dynamic and rewarding practice that requires careful planning, meticulous management, and a deep understanding of bee biology and environmental interactions. By following best practices in preparation, transportation, site selection, hive management, and record keeping, beekeepers can optimize the health and productivity of their colonies while providing essential pollination services and contributing to agricultural sustainability. Adapting to challenges and engaging with local communities further enhances the success and impact of migratory beekeeping operations. Through dedication and continuous learning, migratory beekeepers can thrive in this demanding yet fulfilling endeavor.

3. Innovative Hive Designs

3.1 Top-Bar Hives

Top-bar hives are an innovative and increasingly popular choice among beekeepers seeking a more natural and sustainable method of beekeeping. Unlike the traditional Langstroth hives, top-bar hives are designed to mimic the natural way bees build their hives in the wild. This section will delve into the structure, benefits, challenges, and management practices associated with top-bar hives, providing you with comprehensive knowledge to decide if this hive design is right for you.

Structure and Design

Top-bar hives are characterized by their horizontal layout, which contrasts with the vertical stacking of boxes in Langstroth hives. The primary component of a top-bar hive is a long, horizontal box, typically made from wood, which houses a series of top bars. These bars rest across the width of the hive and serve as the foundation upon which bees build their combs.

- Hive Body: The body of a top-bar hive is a rectangular or trapezoidal box, often with sloping sides to aid in the attachment of the comb to the top bars. The length of the hive can vary, but it is usually between 3 to 4 feet long, providing ample space for the colony to expand horizontally.

- Top Bars: Each top bar is a wooden strip, usually around 1.25 inches wide, that sits across the top of the hive body. Bees build their comb downward from these bars, creating a natural, hanging comb structure. Unlike frames in Langstroth hives, top bars do not have side supports, allowing bees to build their combs with more freedom.

- Entrance: The entrance to the hive is typically a small gap or series of holes at one end of the hive, which helps to minimize drafts and provides a defensible entrance for the bees.

- Roof and Legs: Many top-bar hives feature a sloped roof to protect the hive from rain and snow. The hive often stands on legs to keep it off the ground, which helps with ventilation and pest control.

Benefits of Top-Bar Hives

Top-bar hives offer several benefits that make them appealing to beekeepers interested in more natural and sustainable beekeeping practices.

- Natural Comb Building: In a top-bar hive, bees are free to build their comb in a natural, unrestricted manner. This can result in stronger, healthier combs that are better suited to the bees' needs.

- Ease of Access: The horizontal layout of top-bar hives makes them easier to access and manage. Beekeepers can inspect one comb at a time without disturbing the rest of the hive, reducing stress on the bees.

- Lower Cost: Top-bar hives are often less expensive to build or purchase than Langstroth hives, as they require fewer materials and less complex construction.

- Less Heavy Lifting: Since top-bar hives do not involve stacking heavy boxes, they are easier to manage for beekeepers who may have difficulty lifting heavy objects.

- Enhanced Hive Health: The natural comb building and reduced stress from inspections can lead to healthier colonies. Bees in top-bar hives often show fewer signs of disease and mite infestations.

Challenges of Top-Bar Hives

While top-bar hives have many advantages, they also present unique challenges that beekeepers must consider.

- Comb Fragility: The natural combs built in top-bar hives can be more fragile than those in framed hives, making them susceptible to breakage during inspections or handling.

- Limited Honey Production: Top-bar hives generally produce less honey compared to Langstroth hives. This is because the bees use more resources to build comb, and the hive design does not facilitate the same level of honey storage.

- Temperature Regulation: The horizontal design can make temperature regulation within the hive more challenging, especially in extreme climates. Insulating the hive and careful positioning can help mitigate this issue.

- Experience Required: Managing a top-bar hive requires a different skill set and understanding compared to traditional hives. New beekeepers may need additional training or mentoring to become proficient in top-bar hive management.

Best Practices for Top-Bar Hive Management

To successfully manage a top-bar hive, beekeepers should adopt specific practices tailored to this hive design.

- Comb Management: Regularly inspect and manage comb to prevent cross-comb formation, where bees connect adjacent combs. Using guides or starter strips on the top bars can encourage straight comb building.

- Harvesting Honey: Harvesting honey from a top-bar hive involves cutting the comb from the top bar. Be sure to leave enough honey for the bees to survive through the winter. This process can be done with minimal disruption by only harvesting combs that are fully capped.

- Swarm Prevention: Monitor the hive for signs of swarming, such as queen cells or crowded conditions. Consider splitting the hive or creating additional space by adding more top bars to prevent swarming.

- Pest and Disease Control: Regularly check for signs of pests and diseases. The natural comb in top-bar hives can make it easier to spot problems early. Utilize organic and sustainable methods for pest and disease control to maintain hive health.

- Seasonal Management: Adjust hive management practices according to the seasons. Provide additional insulation during winter and ensure adequate ventilation during hot months. Monitor food stores and supplement with sugar syrup if necessary.

Case Studies and Real-World Examples

To illustrate the practical application of top-bar hives, here are a few case studies from beekeepers who have successfully implemented this hive design.

Case Study 1: Urban Beekeeping in London

Sarah, an urban beekeeper in London, transitioned to top-bar hives to better align with her sustainable lifestyle. She found that the ease of access and minimal disturbance to the bees were significant advantages in her small garden. Despite initial challenges with comb fragility, she quickly learned to handle the combs with care. Her bees thrived, showing improved health and reduced mite infestations compared to her previous Langstroth hives.

Case Study 2: Small-Scale Farm in Oregon

John, a small-scale farmer in Oregon, incorporated top-bar hives into his permaculture farm. The lower cost and simpler design were appealing, and he appreciated the bees' natural comb-building process. He reported a noticeable improvement in pollination of his crops and found the hives easier to manage without heavy lifting. While his honey yield was lower, the quality of the honey and the health of his bees were excellent.

Case Study 3: Educational Apiary in Kenya

A community project in Kenya used top-bar hives to teach local farmers sustainable beekeeping practices. The horizontal design was well-suited to the local environment and materials, and the lower cost made beekeeping accessible to more people. The project saw significant success, with participants able to improve their livelihoods through honey production while maintaining healthy bee populations.

Future Trends in Top-Bar Hive Beekeeping

As interest in sustainable and natural beekeeping continues to grow, the use of top-bar hives is likely to increase. Future trends may include:

- Innovative Materials: Exploring new materials that enhance the durability and insulation of top-bar hives while remaining sustainable and environmentally friendly.

- Technology Integration: Incorporating technology such as sensors and monitoring devices to track hive health and environmental conditions, providing beekeepers with real-time data to make informed decisions.

- Community and Education: Expanding educational programs and community initiatives to promote top-bar hive beekeeping, particularly in regions where traditional beekeeping practices are less accessible.

- Research and Development: Conducting more research on the benefits and challenges of top-bar hives to develop best practices and improve hive designs for various climates and environments.

Conclusion

Top-bar hives offer a unique and sustainable approach to beekeeping that aligns with natural bee behaviors and promotes colony health. While they present certain challenges, with proper management and understanding, top-bar hives can be a rewarding and effective choice for beekeepers of all levels. By embracing innovative hive designs like the top-bar hive, beekeepers can contribute to a more sustainable future for both bees and the environment.

3.2 Warre Hives

The Warre hive, often referred to as the "People's Hive," was developed by French monk Abbé Émile Warré in the early 20th century. His goal was to create a hive that closely mimicked the natural living conditions of bees, thereby promoting their health and productivity. The Warre hive stands out due to its simplicity, affordability, and bee-centric design, making it an excellent choice for both novice and experienced beekeepers who prioritize natural beekeeping practices.

Design and Structure

The Warre hive consists of a series of stacked boxes, each containing fixed, top bars onto which bees build their comb. Unlike the Langstroth hive, the Warre hive does not use frames, which allows bees to construct their comb naturally. This design is closer to the bees' natural environment, as it mimics the vertical cavities found in trees where wild colonies often reside.

Each Warre hive box is typically square and slightly smaller than a Langstroth box, measuring around 12 inches by 12 inches. The standard height of a Warre box is about 8 inches. The boxes are stacked vertically, and new boxes are added at the bottom of the stack (nadiring), encouraging bees to build downwards, similar to their natural behavior in the wild.

The roof of the Warre hive is designed to provide excellent insulation and ventilation. It usually features a quilt box, which is filled with insulating material like wood shavings or straw, and a peaked roof that protects the hive from the elements. This insulation helps maintain a stable internal temperature and humidity, crucial for the bees' health and productivity.

Natural Comb Building

One of the key benefits of the Warre hive is its encouragement of natural comb building. Without frames, bees can build comb in a way that suits their needs, creating cells of varying sizes for brood rearing and honey storage. This natural comb construction can enhance colony health, as it allows bees to regulate their hive environment more effectively.

Natural comb also means less interference from the beekeeper, which can reduce stress on the colony. Additionally, the absence of frames simplifies hive construction and reduces costs, making beekeeping more accessible to a wider audience.

Thermal Regulation and Insulation

The design of the Warre hive emphasizes insulation and thermal regulation. The quilt box and peaked roof provide excellent protection against temperature fluctuations, which is critical for maintaining colony health. In winter, the insulation helps retain heat, reducing the bees' need to consume large amounts of honey to stay warm. In summer, the ventilation provided by the design helps prevent overheating.

This focus on thermal regulation mimics the bees' natural habitat, where they choose tree cavities with thick walls that offer similar insulating properties. By providing a stable environment, the Warre hive helps reduce the stress on bees, leading to healthier and more productive colonies.

Management and Maintenance

Management of a Warre hive is relatively straightforward, which is part of its appeal. The nadiring method of adding new boxes at the bottom requires minimal disturbance to the hive, as opposed to the more invasive process of adding boxes on top in Langstroth hives. This approach respects the bees' natural tendency to expand their hive downward.

Harvesting honey from a Warre hive is also less disruptive. Honey is typically harvested from the upper boxes, which the bees naturally fill with honey stores. Since the lower boxes are used primarily for brood rearing, removing the upper boxes for honey harvest avoids disturbing the brood nest. This method aligns with the philosophy of minimal interference, allowing bees to operate as naturally as possible.

Challenges and Considerations

While the Warre hive offers many benefits, it also presents some challenges. One of the main issues is the difficulty in inspecting individual combs. Because the comb is fixed to the top bars and not housed within removable frames, it is not possible to inspect each comb without cutting it out. This makes it harder to monitor for diseases and pests, a critical aspect of modern beekeeping.

Additionally, because the hive is vertically oriented and boxes are added at the bottom, it can be physically challenging to manage, especially when the hive grows tall. Lifting heavy boxes to add new ones underneath can be cumbersome and may require additional equipment or assistance.

Adapting to Local Conditions

Beekeepers using Warre hives must also consider their local climate and conditions. The hive's design is particularly well-suited for temperate climates with significant seasonal changes. However, in very hot or very cold climates, additional modifications or management strategies might be necessary to ensure the bees thrive.

For instance, in extremely hot climates, additional ventilation may be needed to prevent overheating. In very cold climates, extra insulation or windbreaks might be required to protect the hive from harsh weather. Adapting the Warre hive to local conditions can help maximize its benefits and ensure a healthy, productive colony.

Community and Resources

The Warre hive has a dedicated following among natural beekeepers, and there are numerous resources available for those interested in adopting this method. Online forums, local beekeeping associations, and various books provide valuable information and support. Sharing experiences and tips with other Warre beekeepers can be particularly helpful, as the community aspect of beekeeping often leads to better practices and innovations.

Conclusion

The Warre hive represents a thoughtful, bee-centric approach to beekeeping that aligns closely with the principles of natural and sustainable agriculture. Its design emphasizes the natural behaviors and needs of bees, promoting their health and productivity while minimizing the beekeeper's intervention. While it does present some challenges, particularly regarding hive inspection and management, the benefits of a more natural, less invasive beekeeping method are significant.

For beekeepers committed to natural practices and the well-being of their bees, the Warre hive offers a compelling alternative to more conventional hive designs. By fostering a deeper understanding of and respect for the natural world, the Warre hive not only supports healthier bees but also contributes to the broader goals of environmental sustainability and biodiversity conservation.

CHAPTER VIII
Troubleshooting and Problem-Solving

1. Common Beekeeping Problems

1.1 Hive Health Issues

Maintaining the health of your hive is critical for successful beekeeping. Healthy bees produce more honey, are more resistant to diseases and pests, and contribute to the overall health of the ecosystem. However, hive health issues can arise for various reasons. This section will delve into common hive health problems, their symptoms, and potential solutions.

1.1.1 Varroa Mite Infestation

One of the most significant threats to honey bee health is the Varroa destructor mite. These parasitic mites attach themselves to adult bees and developing brood, sucking their bodily fluids and weakening the bees. Infestations can lead to a variety of problems, including the transmission of viruses, reduced bee lifespan, and colony collapse.

Symptoms:

- Presence of mites on adult bees, visible to the naked eye.

- Deformed wings and abdomens in adult bees.

- Reduced brood production and patchy brood patterns.

- High mite counts in sugar roll or alcohol wash tests.

Solutions:

- Regular monitoring using sugar rolls, alcohol washes, or sticky boards to assess mite levels.

- Integrated Pest Management (IPM) strategies, including the use of miticides like Apivar (amitraz), Apiguard (thymol), or oxalic acid.

- Non-chemical methods such as drone brood removal, which involves removing and destroying drone comb to reduce mite reproduction.

- Breeding and using Varroa-resistant bee strains.

1.1.2 Nosema Disease

Nosema disease, caused by Nosema apis or Nosema ceranae, is a fungal infection that affects the digestive tract of adult bees. It can lead to dysentery, reduced lifespan, and weakened colonies.

Symptoms:

- Brown streaks of feces on the outside of the hive.

- Bees crawling around the hive entrance, unable to fly.

- Reduced honey production and population decline.

- Microscopic examination revealing Nosema spores in bee samples.

Solutions:

- Maintain good hive hygiene and sanitation.

- Provide bees with a healthy diet and clean water sources.

- Treat infected colonies with fumagillin, following the recommended dosage and application guidelines.

- Consider replacing old comb regularly to reduce spore buildup.

1.1.3 American Foulbrood (AFB) and European Foulbrood (EFB)

American Foulbrood (AFB) and European Foulbrood (EFB) are bacterial infections that affect bee larvae. AFB, caused by Paenibacillus larvae, is highly contagious and often fatal, while EFB, caused by Melissococcus plutonius, is less severe but still problematic.

Symptoms of AFB:

- Dead larvae turning dark brown and developing a foul odor.

- Sunken and perforated capped brood cells.

- Presence of "ropiness" – a sticky thread-like substance when dead larvae are probed.

- Hardened scale formation in brood cells.

Symptoms of EFB:

- Larvae twisted in their cells with a yellowish appearance.

- Foul-smelling brood.

- Larvae that die before being capped, often appearing melted or discolored.

Solutions for AFB:

- Immediate burning of infected hives and equipment to prevent the spread.

- Use of antibiotics like oxytetracycline under veterinary guidance.

- Regular inspections and prompt removal of suspect colonies.

Solutions for EFB:

- Improve colony nutrition by providing supplemental feeding.

- Use of oxytetracycline or other antibiotics as recommended.

- Requeening the hive with resistant stock.

1.1.4 Chalkbrood

Chalkbrood is a fungal disease caused by Ascosphaera apis, which affects bee larvae. The fungus grows in the gut of the larvae, eventually turning them into hard, white or grey mummies.

Symptoms:

- Chalk-like mummified larvae in brood cells.

- Mummified larvae often found at the hive entrance.

Solutions:

- Maintain strong, healthy colonies with good ventilation.

- Remove and destroy infected larvae and brood comb.

- Replace old brood comb regularly.

- Ensure proper hive placement to avoid damp, poorly ventilated locations.

1.1.5 Colony Collapse Disorder (CCD)

Colony Collapse Disorder (CCD) is a complex phenomenon where the majority of worker bees in a colony disappear, leaving behind a queen, food stores, and a few nurse bees. The exact cause is still under investigation, but it is believed to be due to a combination of factors including pests, diseases, pesticides, and environmental stressors.

Symptoms:

- Sudden disappearance of the majority of adult bees.

- Presence of a queen and brood, with no dead bees in or around the hive.

- Abandoned food stores.

Solutions:

- Practice good hive management to reduce stress.

- Monitor and control Varroa mite levels and other pests.

- Avoid using pesticides harmful to bees.

- Provide a diverse forage environment to improve bee nutrition.

1.1.6 Parasitic Mite Syndrome (PMS)

Parasitic Mite Syndrome (PMS) is a condition often associated with high levels of Varroa mites. It can result in the decline of the bee population and poor brood patterns.

Symptoms:

- Spotty brood pattern with discolored, sunken cappings.

- Presence of dead or dying larvae.

- Deformed adult bees and high mite loads.

Solutions:

- Regular mite monitoring and management practices.

- Use of IPM strategies to keep mite levels under control.

- Providing bees with adequate nutrition and reducing stressors.

1.1.7 Deformed Wing Virus (DWV)

Deformed Wing Virus (DWV) is closely associated with Varroa mite infestations. The virus causes deformities in developing bees, primarily affecting their wings.

Symptoms:

- Bees with crumpled or deformed wings.

- Reduced bee lifespan and colony population decline.

- Presence of Varroa mites.

Solutions:

- Control Varroa mite populations to reduce the spread of DWV.

- Implement IPM strategies and chemical treatments as necessary.

- Maintain strong, healthy colonies through good management practices.

1.1.8 Small Hive Beetle (SHB) Infestation

Small Hive Beetles (SHB) are pests that can cause significant damage to honey bee colonies. They lay eggs in the hive, and the larvae feed on pollen, honey, and brood, causing fermentation and destruction.

Symptoms:

- Presence of adult beetles and larvae in the hive.

- Fermented honey with a slimy appearance and foul odor.

- Damaged comb and brood cells.

Solutions:

- Use beetle traps and screens to reduce SHB populations.

- Maintain strong colonies to defend against beetle infestations.

- Regularly inspect and clean hives, removing debris and infested comb.

1.1.9 Wax Moth Infestation

Wax moths, particularly the greater wax moth (Galleria mellonella), can cause extensive damage to hives by tunneling through wax comb, leaving webs and debris.

Symptoms:

- Webbing and tunnels in comb.

- Presence of moth larvae and cocoons.

- Damage to wooden hive components.

Solutions:

- Store unused combs in a cool, dry place to prevent moth infestations.

- Use traps and biological controls like Bacillus thuringiensis (Bt) to manage wax moths.

- Maintain strong colonies that can defend against moth invasions.

In conclusion, maintaining hive health requires vigilance, regular inspections, and prompt intervention when problems are identified. By understanding common hive health issues and their solutions, beekeepers can take proactive steps to ensure the well-being of their bees and the success of their beekeeping endeavors.

1.2 Environmental Challenges

Beekeeping, while rewarding, is inherently subject to various environmental challenges that can significantly impact hive health and productivity. Understanding these challenges and how to mitigate them is crucial for any beekeeper aiming to maintain a thriving colony.

1.2.1 Weather Extremes

Hot Weather: Excessive heat can cause bees to become stressed, leading to a decrease in their productivity and overall health. During hot weather, bees work harder to cool the hive, often seen fanning their wings at the entrance to create airflow. To help bees manage high temperatures, ensure adequate ventilation within the hive and consider providing a water source nearby. Additionally, shading the hive during the hottest parts of the day can prevent overheating.

Cold Weather: Cold weather poses a significant threat to bee colonies, especially in regions with harsh winters. Bees cluster together to generate heat, relying on their honey stores for energy. To protect your hive during winter, ensure it is well-insulated but still ventilated to prevent moisture buildup, which can lead to mold and other health issues. Winter feeding might also be necessary if honey stores are insufficient.

1.2.2 Seasonal Variability

Spring: Spring is a critical time for bees as they emerge from winter and begin foraging. A sudden cold snap can kill early flowers, reducing the availability of nectar and pollen. Beekeepers should monitor weather forecasts and, if necessary, provide supplemental feeding to support the colony until natural food sources become available.

Summer: Summer brings an abundance of forage but also the risk of drought. During prolonged dry spells, flowers may produce less nectar, impacting honey production. Ensuring a water source is available and considering planting drought-resistant forage can help sustain bees during these periods.

Fall: Fall is preparation time for winter. Bees need to build up their honey stores, and any early frost can cut short their foraging season. Regular hive inspections are crucial to assess honey reserves and the overall health of the colony. Fall feeding might be necessary to ensure the bees have enough food to survive the winter.

Winter: As mentioned, winter requires careful preparation. In addition to insulation and feeding, beekeepers should also ensure the hive entrance remains clear of snow and ice to allow for proper ventilation and occasional cleansing flights.

1.2.3 Natural Disasters

Floods: Flooding can devastate bee colonies, especially if hives are not elevated. In flood-prone areas, beekeepers should place hives on stands or platforms to keep them above potential water levels. After a flood, it's essential to inspect hives for damage and contamination, and provide immediate care to affected colonies.

Wildfires: Wildfires pose a direct threat to hives and forage areas. Beekeepers in fire-prone regions should have an evacuation plan for their hives. This might include relocating them to a safer area or creating firebreaks around the apiary. After a fire, the availability of forage can be significantly reduced, necessitating supplemental feeding and careful monitoring of the bees' health.

Storms: Severe storms can damage hives and disrupt bee activity. Secure hives with straps or weights to prevent them from being toppled by strong winds. After a storm, check for structural damage and ensure the bees have access to food and water, as foraging may be temporarily disrupted.

1.2.4 Agricultural Practices

Pesticides: Pesticide exposure is one of the most significant environmental challenges facing bees. Insecticides, herbicides, and fungicides can all negatively impact bee health, leading to reduced foraging efficiency, impaired development, and even colony collapse. Beekeepers should communicate with local farmers to understand pesticide application schedules and advocate for bee-friendly practices, such as applying chemicals during times when bees are not active.

Monoculture Farming: Large-scale monoculture farming reduces the diversity of forage available to bees, impacting their nutrition and health. Beekeepers can mitigate this by planting a variety of flowers and plants that bloom at different times, ensuring a continuous food supply. Encouraging local farmers to incorporate pollinator strips or wildflower areas can also benefit bee populations.

Genetically Modified Crops: Some genetically modified (GM) crops are designed to be pest-resistant, which can indirectly affect bees. While the impact of GM crops on bees is still a subject of research, beekeepers should stay informed about developments in agricultural biotechnology and advocate for practices that protect bee health.

1.2.5 Urbanization

Habitat Loss: Urban development often leads to the destruction of natural habitats, reducing the availability of forage and nesting sites for bees. Urban beekeepers can help mitigate this by creating pollinator-friendly gardens and green spaces. Rooftop gardens, community gardens, and even window boxes with flowers can provide vital resources for urban bees.

Pollution: Air and water pollution can impact bee health and the quality of their forage. Urban beekeepers should monitor the local environment for potential pollution sources and advocate for cleaner, greener urban planning. Bees in polluted areas may require more frequent health checks and supplemental feeding to ensure they remain healthy.

Heat Islands: Urban areas often experience higher temperatures than surrounding rural areas due to the heat island effect. This can exacerbate the challenges of hot weather for urban bees. Providing shade, water, and ensuring proper hive ventilation are critical strategies for managing urban hives in hot conditions.

1.2.6 Climate Change

Climate change is an overarching environmental challenge that exacerbates many of the issues discussed above. Changing weather patterns, increased frequency of extreme weather events, and shifting blooming times for plants all impact bee health and productivity.

Shifting Bloom Times: As temperatures rise, plants may bloom earlier or later than usual, disrupting the synchrony between bees and their forage. Beekeepers need to closely monitor local flora and adjust their management practices accordingly. This might include planting a variety of species to ensure continuous forage availability.

Increased Pest and Disease Pressure: Warmer temperatures and changing climates can lead to the proliferation of pests and diseases that affect bees. Beekeepers need to stay vigilant, regularly inspect their hives, and employ integrated pest management (IPM) strategies to keep their colonies healthy.

Resource Management: Climate change can also impact the availability of water and other resources. Beekeepers should consider implementing water conservation practices and ensuring their bees have access to clean, reliable water sources throughout the year.

In conclusion, environmental challenges are a significant aspect of beekeeping that requires careful consideration and proactive management. By understanding the various factors that can impact hive health and implementing strategies to mitigate these challenges, beekeepers can help ensure their colonies remain healthy and productive. Continuous learning, adaptation, and collaboration with other beekeepers and stakeholders are key to overcoming these environmental hurdles and promoting a sustainable future for beekeeping.

2. Pest and Predator Management

2.1 Identifying Threats

Identifying and understanding potential threats to your beehives is crucial for effective pest and predator management. By recognizing the signs of infestation or predation early on, beekeepers can take proactive measures to mitigate risks and protect their colonies. This section will explore the most common threats to beehives, ranging from insects and animals to environmental factors.

2.1.1 Insect Pests

Insects pose significant threats to bee colonies, often preying on bees themselves or compromising hive integrity. Understanding the behavior and characteristics of these pests is essential for successful management.

Varroa Destructor (Varroa Mite)

One of the most notorious threats to honeybee colonies worldwide is the Varroa destructor, commonly known as the Varroa mite. These external parasites feed on the bodily fluids of adult bees and their developing brood, weakening the bees and transmitting various viruses. Identifying a Varroa mite infestation typically involves monitoring for signs such as deformed wings, weakened bees, and the presence of mites on adult bees or within brood cells.

Small Hive Beetle (Aethina Tumida)

Originating from sub-Saharan Africa, the small hive beetle has become a significant concern for beekeepers in many regions. Adult beetles lay their eggs in beehives, and the larvae feed on pollen, honey, and bee brood, ultimately causing hive disruption and deterioration. Signs of a small hive beetle infestation include the presence of adult beetles, slime trails, and damaged comb.

Wax Moths

Wax moths, including the greater wax moth (Galleria mellonella) and the lesser wax moth (Achroia grisella), are common pests in beehives, particularly in weakened or neglected colonies. These moths lay their eggs in hive crevices, and their larvae consume beeswax, pollen, and bee brood. Beekeepers may detect wax moth infestations through the presence of webbing, cocoons, or damaged comb.

Ants

While ants may seem relatively innocuous compared to other pests, they can still pose a threat to beehives, especially weaker colonies. Ants may infiltrate hives in search of food or shelter, disrupting hive activities and potentially causing bee losses. Beekeepers should be vigilant for ant trails leading to hive entrances and take measures to prevent ant access, such as using hive stands with integrated ant barriers or applying deterrents around hive bases.

2.1.2 Animal Predators

Various animals, ranging from mammals to birds and reptiles, may target beehives as a food source or nesting site. Managing these predators requires a combination of deterrents, habitat modification, and protective measures.

Bears

In regions where bears are present, beekeepers face the constant threat of hive destruction. Bears are attracted to the scent of honey and will readily tear apart hives to access it. Electric fencing is often used as a deterrent against bears, as they are sensitive to electric shocks. Additionally, securing hives with bear-proof enclosures or relocating them to bear-safe areas can help minimize losses.

Skunks

Skunks are opportunistic feeders that may target beehives, particularly during times of scarcity. They are known to scratch at hive entrances to dislodge bees and consume honey or brood. To deter skunks, beekeepers can install entrance reducers or place wire mesh around hive stands to prevent access. Additionally, removing attractants such as fallen fruit or garbage can help reduce skunk activity near apiaries.

Raccoons

Raccoons are skilled climbers and can easily access elevated hives, making them formidable adversaries for beekeepers. These nocturnal mammals may raid beehives in search of honey, brood, or bees. To protect against raccoon predation, beekeepers can install electric fencing or use hardware cloth to reinforce hive stands and entrances. Removing potential food sources and securing hive components can also deter raccoons from targeting apiaries.

Birds

Certain bird species, such as woodpeckers and European starlings, may cause damage to beehives by pecking at wooden components or attempting to access hive contents. To deter birds, beekeepers can utilize visual deterrents such as reflective tape or predator decoys. Placing netting or wire mesh over hives can also prevent birds from causing harm while still allowing bees to enter and exit freely.

2.1.3 Environmental Factors

In addition to pests and predators, environmental factors can also impact bee colonies, affecting their health and productivity. Understanding these influences is essential for beekeepers seeking to maintain thriving apiaries.

Climate Extremes

Extreme weather events, such as heatwaves, cold snaps, and heavy rainfall, can stress bee colonies and disrupt their normal activities. Beekeepers should monitor weather forecasts and take preemptive measures to protect hives during adverse conditions, such as providing supplemental feeding, insulating hives, or providing shade.

Pesticide Exposure

Exposure to pesticides is a significant concern for beekeepers, as certain chemicals can have detrimental effects on bee health and behavior. Bees may encounter pesticides through contaminated pollen, nectar, or water sources, leading to acute or chronic toxicity. To minimize pesticide exposure, beekeepers should communicate with neighboring farmers and landscapers to encourage the use of bee-friendly practices and establish buffer zones between apiaries and pesticide-treated areas.

Habitat Loss

Loss of floral resources due to habitat destruction or land-use changes can limit bee foraging opportunities and negatively impact colony nutrition. Beekeepers can mitigate habitat loss by planting bee-friendly flora, providing diverse forage options throughout the growing season, and advocating for conservation efforts to protect natural habitats.

Conclusion

Identifying and addressing potential threats to bee colonies is essential for maintaining healthy and productive apiaries. By staying vigilant, implementing preventive measures, and responding promptly to signs of trouble, beekeepers can effectively manage pest and predator pressures and safeguard their hives against environmental challenges. Through continuous monitoring and proactive management practices, beekeepers can contribute to the resilience and sustainability of honeybee populations worldwide.

2.2 Prevention and Control

Preventing and controlling pests and predators is a crucial aspect of successful beekeeping. Left unchecked, these threats can decimate bee populations and jeopardize the health of entire colonies. However, with proactive measures and strategic management techniques, beekeepers can mitigate risks and safeguard their hives. In this section, we will explore effective strategies for preventing and controlling pests and predators in beekeeping operations.

Integrated Pest Management (IPM)

Integrated Pest Management (IPM) is a holistic approach to pest control that emphasizes prevention, monitoring, and targeted intervention. Instead of relying solely on chemical pesticides, IPM integrates various methods to manage pests in an environmentally responsible manner. In beekeeping, IPM strategies include cultural, biological, and mechanical controls to minimize the use of synthetic chemicals and reduce negative impacts on bee health and the environment.

Cultural Controls

Cultural controls involve practices that manipulate the beekeeping environment to discourage pest activity and promote bee colony resilience. Some cultural control methods include:

1. Hygienic Beekeeping Practices: Maintaining a clean and well-organized apiary can help reduce pest attraction and reproduction. Regularly removing debris, old comb, and other hive materials can prevent the buildup of pests such as wax moths and small hive beetles.

2. Apiary Location Selection: Choosing an appropriate location for bee hives can influence pest exposure. Avoiding areas with known pest infestations or selecting sites with good airflow and sunlight can help deter pests and promote colony health.

3. Proper Hive Management: Regular hive inspections and maintenance are essential for early pest detection and intervention. Monitoring hive conditions, population levels, and behavior can help beekeepers identify potential pest problems before they escalate.

Biological Controls

Biological controls utilize natural predators, parasites, and pathogens to regulate pest populations without the need for chemical interventions. By harnessing the power of beneficial organisms, beekeepers can effectively manage pests while minimizing harm to bees and the environment. Some biological control methods include:

1. Predatory Insects: Introducing or encouraging natural predators of hive pests, such as predatory mites or certain beetle species, can help keep pest populations in check. However, care must be taken to ensure that introduced predators do not become pests themselves or harm beneficial insects.

2. Parasitic Mites: Certain mite species, such as the varroa mite, can devastate bee colonies if left unchecked. Biological control methods for varroa mites include the use of parasitic mite species that specifically target varroa populations without harming bees.

3. Pathogenic Microorganisms: Beneficial microorganisms, such as certain bacteria and fungi, can be used to control pest populations by infecting and weakening target organisms. Biopesticides derived from naturally occurring pathogens offer a sustainable alternative to chemical pesticides.

Mechanical Controls

Mechanical controls involve physical barriers or devices designed to exclude or trap pests and predators. These methods can be effective in preventing pest access to bee hives and reducing infestation risks. Some mechanical control techniques include:

1. Entrance Reducers: Installing entrance reducers or guards can limit the entry of larger pests, such as rodents or birds, while still allowing bees to come and go freely. Entrance reducers can also help bees defend against intruders by narrowing the hive entrance.

2. Screened Bottom Boards: Using screened bottom boards in hive configurations can prevent pests, such as varroa mites or small hive beetles, from gaining access to the hive interior. Screened bottom boards allow debris to fall through while providing ventilation and reducing moisture buildup.

3. Traps and Barriers: Placing traps or barriers around hives can intercept pests and prevent them from reaching bee colonies. Trap designs vary depending on the target pest, with options including sticky traps, baited traps, and physical barriers made of materials like wire mesh or plastic.

Chemical Controls

While minimizing chemical interventions is ideal for beekeeping sustainability, there are situations where targeted pesticide applications may be necessary to manage severe pest infestations. When using chemical controls, beekeepers must prioritize the safety of bees, humans, and the environment by selecting products approved for use in beekeeping and following label instructions carefully. Some considerations for chemical pest control include:

1. Selective Pesticides: Choose pesticides that specifically target the pest species of concern while minimizing harm to non-target organisms, including bees and beneficial insects. Selective pesticides with low toxicity to bees, such as those based on natural compounds or insect growth regulators, are preferable.

2. Timing and Application Methods: Apply pesticides during periods of minimal bee activity, such as early morning or late evening, to reduce direct exposure to foraging bees. Use targeted application methods, such as spot treatments or localized applications, to minimize pesticide drift and off-target effects.

3. Monitoring and Resistance Management: Regularly monitor pest populations and assess the effectiveness of chemical control measures to avoid over-reliance on pesticides and minimize the risk of resistance development. Rotate pesticide classes and use integrated approaches to maintain long-term pest control efficacy.

Conclusion

Preventing and controlling pests and predators is an ongoing challenge for beekeepers, but with proactive management strategies and a commitment to sustainability, it is possible to maintain healthy and productive bee colonies. By adopting integrated pest management techniques that emphasize prevention, monitoring, and targeted intervention, beekeepers can minimize reliance on chemical pesticides and promote the long-term health and viability of their apiaries. Through a combination of cultural, biological, mechanical, and chemical controls, beekeepers can effectively manage pest and predator pressures while supporting thriving bee populations and sustainable beekeeping practices.

Conclusion

1. The Future of Beekeeping

As we delve into the future of beekeeping, it becomes evident that the fate of these vital pollinators lies at the intersection of environmental conservation, technological innovation, and human stewardship. In this chapter, we will explore the challenges and opportunities that await beekeepers in the coming years, along with the evolving role of beekeeping in sustaining both ecosystems and food security.

1. Embracing Sustainable Practices

Sustainability is the cornerstone of future beekeeping endeavors. With environmental pressures mounting and bee populations dwindling, beekeepers must prioritize practices that promote the health and well-being of their colonies while minimizing negative impacts on the surrounding ecosystem. This entails adopting organic and natural beekeeping methods, reducing reliance on chemical inputs, and implementing habitat restoration initiatives to provide bees with diverse forage sources.

2. Harnessing Technology for Hive Management

Advancements in technology offer unprecedented opportunities for hive monitoring and management. From IoT (Internet of Things) sensors that track hive conditions in real-time to AI-powered analytics that predict disease outbreaks, beekeepers now have access to a suite of tools that can revolutionize their approach to beekeeping. By leveraging these technologies, beekeepers can detect early signs of stress or disease, optimize hive productivity, and make data-driven decisions to enhance colony health.

3. Addressing Pesticide Use and Habitat Loss

The widespread use of pesticides and habitat loss pose significant threats to bee populations worldwide. To safeguard the future of beekeeping, concerted efforts are needed to mitigate these challenges. This involves advocating for stricter regulations on pesticide usage, promoting the adoption of bee-friendly farming practices, and actively participating in habitat restoration initiatives. By working collaboratively with policymakers, farmers, and conservationists, beekeepers can help create landscapes that are conducive to bee health and biodiversity.

4. Educating and Engaging the Public

Public awareness and education play a crucial role in shaping the future of beekeeping. As stewards of these invaluable pollinators, beekeepers have a responsibility to share their knowledge and passion with the broader community. By organizing workshops, hosting educational events, and partnering with schools and local organizations, beekeepers can inspire the next generation of environmentalists and foster a deeper appreciation for the importance of bees in our ecosystem.

5. Adapting to Climate Change

Climate change poses complex challenges for beekeepers, affecting everything from floral bloom times to the prevalence of pests and diseases. In the face of these changes, beekeepers must remain adaptable and resilient. This may involve diversifying beekeeping practices, selecting bee breeds that are better suited to changing environmental conditions, and implementing strategies to mitigate heat stress and other climate-related risks. By embracing innovative solutions and collaborating with researchers and climate scientists, beekeepers can navigate the challenges of a rapidly changing climate.

6. Promoting Diversity and Inclusivity

Diversity and inclusivity are essential for the long-term sustainability of beekeeping. Historically, beekeeping has been predominantly male-dominated, but efforts are underway to promote greater gender and cultural diversity within the beekeeping community. By creating inclusive spaces and providing support and resources to underrepresented beekeepers, we can harness the diverse perspectives and experiences needed to address the complex challenges facing bees and beekeepers alike.

Conclusion: A Call to Action

As we peer into the future of beekeeping, one thing is clear: the stakes have never been higher. The fate of bees is intricately linked to the health of our planet, and beekeepers have a crucial role to play in shaping that future. By embracing sustainable practices, harnessing technology, advocating for policy change, educating the public, adapting to a changing climate, and promoting diversity and inclusivity, we can build a future where bees thrive and beekeeping remains a vibrant and essential component of our agricultural landscape. The time to act is now. Together, let us embark on this journey to ensure a bee-friendly future for generations to come.

2. Continuing Your Beekeeping Journey

Congratulations on completing the journey through the pages of "Bee-Friendly: A Comprehensive Guide to Home Beekeeping"! As you embark on the next phase of your beekeeping adventure, this section aims to provide you with further guidance and resources to continue nurturing your passion for bees and beekeeping.

1. Expanding Your Apiary

Now that you've gained experience with beekeeping, you might be considering expanding your apiary. Before you do so, take the time to evaluate your current setup. Are your bees thriving in their environment? Do you have sufficient knowledge and resources to manage additional hives? Assessing these factors will help you make informed decisions about expanding your beekeeping operation.

When adding new hives, consider factors such as hive placement, spacing between hives, and the availability of forage in the surrounding area. Proper planning will contribute to the success and health of your bees.

2. Diversifying Your Beekeeping Skills

Beekeeping is a multifaceted hobby with numerous areas to explore. Consider diversifying your beekeeping skills by delving into topics such as queen rearing, honey extraction techniques, or natural pest management strategies. By expanding your knowledge and skillset, you'll become a more well-rounded beekeeper capable of addressing various challenges that may arise.

Additionally, consider attending beekeeping workshops, seminars, or conferences. These events provide valuable opportunities to learn from experienced beekeepers, exchange ideas, and stay updated on the latest advancements in beekeeping practices.

3. Contributing to Bee Conservation Efforts

As a beekeeper, you play a vital role in bee conservation efforts. Beyond caring for your own hives, consider ways to contribute to the preservation of bee populations and their habitats. This could involve participating in citizen science projects, planting bee-friendly flora in your community, or advocating for policies that support pollinator health.

By actively engaging in bee conservation initiatives, you'll not only help protect bees but also raise awareness about the importance of these remarkable creatures to our ecosystem.

4. Sharing Your Knowledge and Passion

One of the most rewarding aspects of beekeeping is sharing your knowledge and passion with others. Whether it's through social media, community workshops, or mentoring aspiring beekeepers, there are numerous ways to inspire and educate others about the fascinating world of bees.

Consider starting a beekeeping blog or YouTube channel to document your experiences and provide valuable insights to fellow bee enthusiasts. You can also offer hive tours or educational presentations to schools, garden clubs, or community groups.

5. Continuing Education and Research

Beekeeping is an ever-evolving field, and there is always more to learn. Stay curious and committed to ongoing education and research. Explore new beekeeping publications, scientific studies, and online forums to stay informed about emerging trends and best practices in beekeeping.

Additionally, consider pursuing formal education opportunities in apiculture through courses offered by universities or agricultural extension programs. Continuing education will deepen your understanding of beekeeping principles and equip you with the knowledge to overcome challenges and optimize hive management.

6. Embracing the Joy of Beekeeping

Above all, remember to embrace the joy and wonder of beekeeping. Whether you're marveling at the intricate dance of bees in flight, savoring the sweet taste of freshly harvested honey, or simply spending time in the company of your buzzing companions, let your love for bees guide you on this fulfilling journey.

As you continue your beekeeping adventure, may you find inspiration in the resilience and beauty of these remarkable creatures. Thank you for your dedication to the well-being of bees, and may your apiary flourish for years to come.

Conclusion

In conclusion, the journey of beekeeping is both rewarding and enriching, offering countless opportunities for learning, growth, and connection with nature. By continuing to expand your apiary, diversify your skills, contribute to bee conservation efforts, share your knowledge, pursue ongoing education, and embrace the joy of beekeeping, you'll cultivate a thriving and sustainable beekeeping practice that benefits both bees and beekeepers alike.

Remember, the world of beekeeping is as vast and diverse as the bees themselves, and there's always something new to discover. So, keep exploring, keep learning, and above all, keep buzzing!

Wishing you continued success and fulfillment on your beekeeping journey. Happy beekeeping!

3. Final Thoughts and Encouragement

As we conclude our journey through the world of beekeeping, it's essential to reflect on the significance of our actions and the impact they have on the environment, our communities, and the future of our planet. Beekeeping is not just a hobby or a profession; it's a vital component of sustainable agriculture, biodiversity, and food security. In this final section, we'll delve deeper into the importance of beekeeping, offer some words of encouragement, and discuss how each of us can contribute to the well-being of bees and our ecosystem.

The Importance of Beekeeping

Throughout this guide, we've emphasized the crucial role that bees play in pollination, ecosystem health, and food production. Bees are not only responsible for pollinating a significant portion of the world's crops but also contribute to the reproduction of countless plant species, including those that provide habitat and food for other wildlife. Without bees, our agricultural systems would collapse, leading to widespread food shortages, economic instability, and environmental degradation.

Beekeeping offers a way to support bee populations while also reaping the benefits of their pollination services. By providing bees with safe habitats, adequate nutrition, and protection from pests and diseases, beekeepers help ensure the health and vitality of bee colonies. Additionally, beekeeping fosters a deeper connection to nature, promotes sustainable practices, and encourages community involvement. Whether you're a backyard beekeeper or a commercial operator, your contributions to beekeeping are invaluable.

Words of Encouragement

Embarking on a journey into beekeeping can be both rewarding and challenging. It requires dedication, patience, and a willingness to learn from both successes and failures. As you navigate the complexities of beekeeping, remember that every beekeeper started as a beginner and faced obstacles along the way. Take comfort in knowing that there is a vast community of beekeepers, researchers, and enthusiasts who are eager to share their knowledge and support your journey.

Be prepared to adapt and evolve as you gain experience and encounter new situations. Beekeeping is a dynamic practice that requires continuous learning and adjustment to changing conditions. Don't be discouraged by setbacks or setbacks; instead, use them as opportunities to grow and improve your skills. Celebrate the successes, no matter how small, and learn from the challenges you face.

Above all, approach beekeeping with reverence and respect for the bees themselves. These remarkable creatures deserve our admiration and protection, and it's our responsibility as stewards of the land to ensure their well-being. Treat your bees with care and compassion, and they will reward you with their industriousness and resilience.

How You Can Make a Difference

As you continue your beekeeping journey, consider how you can make a positive impact on bee health and conservation efforts. Here are some actions you can take:

1. Plant Bee-Friendly Gardens: Create a diverse habitat for bees by planting a variety of flowers, shrubs, and trees that provide nectar and pollen throughout the year. Choose native plant species whenever possible, as they are best adapted to your local ecosystem.

2. Avoid Pesticides: Minimize the use of pesticides and herbicides in your garden and yard, as these chemicals can harm bees and other beneficial insects. Instead, opt for natural pest control methods and integrated pest management techniques.

3. Support Local Beekeepers: Purchase honey and other bee products from local beekeepers who practice sustainable beekeeping methods. By supporting local beekeepers, you help ensure the viability of beekeeping as a livelihood and promote bee-friendly practices in your community.

4. Educate Others: Share your knowledge and passion for beekeeping with friends, family, and neighbors. Help raise awareness about the importance of bees and the threats they face, and inspire others to take action to protect them.

5. Get Involved: Consider volunteering with local beekeeping associations, conservation organizations, or community gardens. By getting involved in bee-related initiatives, you can make a meaningful contribution to bee health and habitat conservation efforts.

Conclusion

As we bring our exploration of beekeeping to a close, I encourage you to approach beekeeping not only as a hobby or a livelihood but as a calling to stewardship and conservation. By caring for bees and their habitats, we not only ensure our own survival but also preserve the intricate web of life that sustains us all. May your journey in beekeeping be filled with wonder, discovery, and the sweet rewards of a thriving hive. Remember, the future of beekeeping lies in our hands, and together, we can create a world where bees and humans thrive in harmony.

Thank you for joining me on this journey, and may your beekeeping adventures be both fulfilling and fruitful. Buzz on, fellow bee enthusiasts, and may the hum of bees forever grace our gardens and fields.

Sincerely,

Appendices

1. Glossary of Beekeeping Terms

Beekeeping, also known as apiculture, encompasses a rich lexicon of terms and jargon specific to the practice of caring for bees and managing hives. Whether you're a novice beekeeper or a seasoned apiarist, understanding these terms is essential for effective communication within the beekeeping community. Below is a comprehensive glossary to help you navigate the world of beekeeping:

1. Apiary: A location where beehives are kept; also referred to as a bee yard.

2. Apiculture: The practice of beekeeping, including the management of honeybees for honey production, pollination, and other benefits.

3. Beehive: A man-made structure designed to house honeybees, typically consisting of stacked boxes containing frames where bees build comb and store honey.

4. Colony: A group of bees living together in a hive, including a queen, workers, and drones.

5. Queen: The female bee responsible for laying eggs and regulating the activities of the colony.

6. Worker: Female bees responsible for various tasks within the hive, including foraging, nursing the brood, and building comb.

7. Drone: Male bees whose primary role is to mate with a queen during her nuptial flight.

8. Comb: The structure built by bees using wax secreted from their glands, used for storing honey, pollen, and raising brood.

9. Frame: A rectangular or square structure within a hive where bees build comb and store honey.

10. Foundation: A sheet of beeswax or plastic with an imprint of honeycomb used as a base for bees to build comb.

11. Honey: A sweet, viscous substance produced by bees from the nectar of flowers and stored in honeycomb.

12. Nectar: A sugary fluid produced by flowers, collected by bees for making honey.

13. Pollen: Fine powder produced by flowers' male reproductive organs, collected by bees as a protein source.

14. Propolis: A resinous substance collected by bees from tree buds and used to seal cracks and reinforce the hive.

15. Swarm: A large group of bees, including a queen and workers, that leaves the hive to establish a new colony.

16. Nucleus Hive (Nuc): A small hive containing a queen and a few frames of bees, used for starting new colonies or rearing queens.

17. Super: An additional box added to the top of a hive for surplus honey storage.

18. Queen Excluder: A device placed between hive boxes to prevent the queen from laying eggs in honey supers.

19. Smoker: A tool used by beekeepers to produce smoke, which calms bees and makes them easier to work with.

20. Veil: Protective clothing worn by beekeepers to prevent bee stings, typically consisting of a mesh hood that covers the head and face.

21. Hive Tool: A specialized tool used by beekeepers to pry apart hive components, remove frames, and scrape propolis.

22. Robbing: When bees from one colony steal honey from another colony's hive.

23. Varroa Destructor: A parasitic mite that infests honeybee colonies, feeding on the bees and transmitting diseases.

24. Queen Rearing: The process of selectively breeding honeybee queens for desirable traits such as docility, productivity, and disease resistance.

25. Honey Extractor: A device used to spin honey out of honeycomb frames, separating the honey from the wax.

26. Feeder: A container used to provide supplemental food, such as sugar syrup, to bees during times of scarcity.

27. Honey Flow: Periods when flowers are abundant and bees collect large amounts of nectar, resulting in increased honey production.

28. Foundationless Frames: Frames within a hive that do not contain pre-formed foundation, allowing bees to build natural comb.

29. Queen Cell: A special cell within the comb where a queen bee is raised from an egg.

30. Swarm Trap: A baited container used to attract and capture swarms of bees, often used by beekeepers to increase their colony numbers.

This glossary provides a foundation for understanding the terminology used in beekeeping. As you continue your journey in apiculture, you'll encounter many more specialized terms and concepts, each adding to your knowledge and appreciation of these remarkable insects and their intricate social structure.

2. Beekeeping Calendar

A successful beekeeping venture relies heavily on timing and seasonality. Understanding the natural rhythms of the hive and the surrounding environment is crucial for beekeepers to effectively manage their colonies and maximize productivity. The beekeeping calendar serves as a guide, outlining key tasks and activities to be performed throughout the year. By adhering to a structured schedule, beekeepers can promote colony health, mitigate potential risks, and optimize honey production. This section provides a comprehensive beekeeping calendar, organized by month, to assist beekeepers in planning and managing their apiaries.

January

- Evaluate Hive Stores: Check the honey stores within the hive to ensure an adequate supply for the colony during the winter months.

- Monitor Hive Weight: Use a scale or hefting method to gauge the weight of the hive. Supplement with additional food if necessary.

- Inspect Hive: On milder days, conduct a brief inspection of the hive to assess colony activity and health.

- Order Equipment and Supplies: Take inventory of beekeeping equipment and order any necessary supplies for the upcoming season.

February

- Prepare Equipment: Clean and repair hive components, including frames, supers, and hive bodies.

- Plan for Swarm Management: Develop a strategy for swarm prevention and management as the colony begins to expand.

- Attend Beekeeping Workshops: Take advantage of educational opportunities and workshops to enhance beekeeping knowledge and skills.

- Monitor Varroa Mite Levels: Implement mite monitoring techniques and plan for appropriate treatment measures.

March

- Perform Hive Inspections: Conduct comprehensive inspections of hive health and brood patterns.

- Begin Feeding: If necessary, supplement hive food stores with sugar syrup or fondant to stimulate brood rearing.

- Split Colonies: Consider splitting strong colonies to prevent swarming and increase hive numbers.

- Monitor Pollen Sources: Identify local flowering plants and trees to track pollen availability for foraging bees.

April

- Expand Hive Space: Add additional supers or hive bodies to accommodate colony growth and prevent overcrowding.

- Check Queen Performance: Evaluate queen performance and consider requeening if necessary to maintain colony vigor.

- Monitor Hive Temperatures: Ensure proper ventilation and insulation to regulate hive temperature during fluctuating spring weather.

- Continue Varroa Mite Management: Implement integrated pest management strategies to control varroa mite infestations.

May

- Harvest Spring Honey: If conditions permit, harvest surplus honey from the hive. Ensure adequate food reserves remain for the colony.

- Monitor Swarming Signs: Watch for signs of swarming activity, such as queen cells or increased bee agitation.

- Monitor Hive Hygiene: Maintain hive cleanliness to prevent disease and pest buildup.

- Plant Bee-Friendly Flowers: Sow seeds or plant flowers that provide nectar and pollen resources for foraging bees.

June

- Conduct Mid-Season Inspection: Perform a thorough examination of hive health, brood patterns, and honey stores.

- Manage Swarm Cells: Remove swarm cells or perform swarm prevention techniques to control colony reproduction.

- Provide Water Sources: Place water containers near the hive to ensure bees have access to clean water for cooling and hydration.

- Monitor Honey Production: Track honey production and prepare for potential honey harvesting later in the season.

July

- Monitor Hive Weight: Assess hive stores and provide supplemental feeding if necessary to support colony growth.

- Control Hive Beetles: Implement management strategies to control small hive beetle populations and prevent damage to hive resources.

- Assess Queen Performance: Evaluate queen performance and consider requeening if productivity declines.

- Monitor Nectar Flows: Monitor local nectar flows and adjust hive management strategies accordingly.

August

- Harvest Summer Honey: Extract honey from supers as the main nectar flow diminishes. Ensure proper processing and storage of harvested honey.

- Prepare for Fall Management: Begin preparations for fall hive management, including pest management and winterization.

- Monitor Hive Health: Watch for signs of disease or pest infestations and take appropriate action as needed.

- Attend Beekeeping Conferences: Participate in beekeeping conferences or events to stay informed about industry trends and best practices.

September

- Assess Colony Strength: Evaluate colony strength and population in preparation for overwintering.

- Treat for Varroa Mites: Administer varroa mite treatments to reduce parasite levels before winter.

- Provide Winter Feed: Ensure hives have an ample supply of food stores to sustain colonies through the winter months.

- Prepare Winter Equipment: Install entrance reducers and insulation to help colonies conserve heat and minimize cold drafts.

October

- Complete Harvest: Finish harvesting any remaining honey and prepare hives for winter storage.

- Reduce Entrance Size: Install entrance reducers to minimize heat loss and deter pests from entering the hive.

- Monitor Hive Weight: Continue monitoring hive weight and provide additional food if necessary.

- Prepare Apiary for Winter: Clean and organize the apiary, removing debris and ensuring hives are securely positioned for winter weather.

November

- Winterize Hives: Wrap hives with insulation or moisture-absorbing materials to protect against cold temperatures and moisture buildup.

- Monitor Hive Entrances: Clear snow and debris from hive entrances to maintain proper ventilation.

- Attend Beekeeping Meetings: Participate in local beekeeping meetings or workshops to exchange knowledge and experiences with other beekeepers.

- Plan for Spring: Review beekeeping practices from the past season and develop plans for improvement in the upcoming year.

December

- Monitor Hive Vitality: Check on hive vitality and activity during winter months, weather permitting.

- Monitor Hive Moisture Levels: Ensure hives remain adequately ventilated to prevent moisture buildup, which can lead to mold and disease.

- Continue Education: Take advantage of the offseason to engage in beekeeping education through reading, online courses, or workshops.

- Prepare Equipment for Spring: Clean and organize beekeeping equipment in preparation for the upcoming spring season.

Conclusion

The beekeeping calendar serves as an indispensable tool for beekeepers, providing guidance and structure throughout the year. By following a systematic schedule of tasks and activities, beekeepers can optimize hive health, honey production, and overall apiary management. However, it's essential to remain flexible and responsive to the ever-changing needs of the hive and surrounding environment. Through careful observation, proactive management, and ongoing education, beekeepers can cultivate thriving bee colonies and contribute to the preservation of these vital pollinators.